Verdict on the Shroud

Evidence for the Death and Resurrection of Jesus Christ

Kenneth E. Stevenson
Gary R. Habermas

SERVANT BOOKS
Ann Arbor, Michigan

Book Design by John B. Leidy

Published by Servant Books, Box 8617,
Ann Arbor, Michigan 48107

Printed in the United States of America

ISBN 0-89283-111-1

Photo Credits

1a, 6, 8, 9, 10, 11, 12, 13, 15, 17, 21, 24, 25, 26, 28 copyright
  © Vernon Miller, Brooks Institute of Photography,
  Santa Barbara

4, 27, 29, 30, 31, 32, 33, 34, 35 copyright © Ernest Brooks,
  Brooks Institute

1b, 2, 3 courtesy of Ian Wilson

18, 23 courtesy of Jean Lorre, Jet Propulsion Laboratory

19, 30 copyright © Mark Evans, Brooks Institute

14, 36 courtesy of Brooks Institute

5 courtesy of Holy Shroud Guild

7 courtesy of Francis L. Filas

16 courtesy of John Jackson and Eric Jumper

22 copyright © Tom Fox, Brooks Institute

Lovingly Dedicated to Mary, Jeep, and Nin

Contents

Foreword

Unfortunately there has been considerable confusion about the purpose of the 1978 scientific investigation of the Shroud of Turin. In the minds of some people, the investigators were merely a group of technically accomplished religious fanatics out to "prove" the Shroud's authenticity. At the other extreme, some news accounts have stated that our goal was to prove it a fake. In fact neither is the case—science must never be applied to prove a point. Our purpose was simply to observe and to learn as much as we could about this remarkable physical object in the limited time and circumstances allotted and then to interpret the results of our study as objectively as possible.

For most people who are interested in the problem, there is but a single question of any importance: Was the Shroud of Turin the actual burial cloth of Jesus Christ, or was it not? For centuries, proponents of authenticity and their opponents have argued the issue. They are likely to continue, for science has not yet and perhaps never will provide the answer. Such is a matter for historians to decide. This is not to say that the scientists have learned nothing at all. On the contrary, we have learned a great deal, and the purpose of this book in part is to present an overview of our present scientific understanding.

The "problem of the Shroud" is truly a multidisciplinary one; experts in such diverse fields as physics, chemistry, medicine, and image processing have all contributed in meaningful ways. Stevenson and Habermas have presented the technical results from these various disciplines as objectively as possible in terms understandable to the layman. Although as a physicist I am only qualified to vouch for their success in the matters concerning the physics and chemistry of the problem, I feel that the reader should finish with some reliable impressions about where we stand generally.

Indeed we have learned a great deal, but we have not learned enough about some questions. How did the image arrive on the cloth? The scientific evidence thus far can prove no theory; we cannot know for sure. However, in this work, Stevenson and Habermas have reexamined the problem in the light of certain historical, philosophical, as well as scientific arguments and have proposed an explanation that involves an intervention of the supernatural. To some people this may be shocking; yet if the authors' hypothesis is consistent with the available evidence, it remains a plausible explanation. Stevenson and Habermas have rightly remained cautious in their interpretation. The reader is asked to keep an open mind but at the same time to remain cautious and critical. We should not refrain from careful conclusions and we draw conclusions in light of these facts.

Lawrence Schwalbe, Ph.D.
Los Alamos National Scientific Laboratory
Physicist, Shroud of Turin Research Project

Part I

The Facts About the Shroud

ONE

The Phenomenon
of the Shroud

ON THE FACE OF it, the Shroud of Turin is an unlikely object for serious scientific study or religious edification. The Shroud is an old linen cloth thought by many Christians to be the burial shroud which Joseph of Arimathea and Nicodemus draped around the body of Jesus before they laid him in the tomb. This seems hardly possible. Furthermore, the cloth is imprinted with an image. To the naked eye, the details of this image are hard to discern. It is ghostly, dim, and it fades into a hazy blur as the viewer approaches the cloth. How plausible is the claim that this is a highly detailed image of Jesus himself as he lay in the tomb?

Yet the Shroud of Turin will not be consigned to the category of colorful but bogus relics such as the crown of thorns, the crucifixion nails, and the rod of Moses. Some medieval bishops were sure that the Shroud was a painting, but a painting is one thing that scientists of the twentieth century who have studied the Shroud are sure that it is not.

The irony of the situation is that the mystery of the Shroud

3

has deepened as scientists have inspected it with ever-more sophisticated instruments. In 1898, when the Shroud was first photographed, the image was found to be a negative: its light and dark values were reversed when it was "printed" on a piece of photographic film. This "print" was far more detailed and lifelike than the original. Then in the mid-1970s, microscopic examination of the cloth failed to turn up any sign of pigment, dye, ink, powder, or any other substance that an artist could have used to paint the image. Also in the mid-1970s, an image analyzer connected to a computer found that the Shroud image contains three-dimensional information, a wholly astounding and unexpected discovery, and one which still has no convincing explanation.

Millions of Christians became intensely interested in the Shroud when the photographs of the negative image were published in books, magazines, and newspapers throughout the world. These photos revealed a crucified body in extraordinary detail. Believers and nonbelievers alike could count the scourge wounds, observe a bloody wound in the man's side, see his pierced wrists and feet, and note the signs of a beating in the face. The man of the Shroud, it seemed, suffered and died very much the way the gospels say Jesus of Nazareth suffered and died.

Thus began the phenomenon of the Shroud. It is very much a twentieth-century phenomenon. The Shroud of Turin was an unexceptional relic until people began to examine it with modern scientific instruments. The result has been a remarkable possibility: the more we learn about the Shroud, the more likely it seems that the cloth is what it purports to be—the burial garment of Jesus Christ.

The phenomenon of the Shroud consists largely of intense reactions to the possibility that the Shroud is genuine. If archaeologists digging in a ruin somewhere in the Mediterranean world had unearthed a cloth imprinted with a mysterious image of some unknown person, the discovery would probably be greeted with a moderate amount of excitement and curiosity. But the Shroud of Turin is said to bear an image of Jesus Christ. Thus people's opinion of the Shroud often reflects what they think about Jesus, rather than calm reflection on the possibility that an object with religious value may have survived since the first century A.D. We should take a closer look at some of these reactions.

A common response to the Shroud is instant disbelief: it *can't* be genuine. At the beginning of the twentieth century, Yves Delage, an eminent professor of anatomy and a well-known agnostic, read a paper to his colleagues in the French Academy in which he concluded that the man of the Shroud was Jesus Christ. He was greeted with derision and outrage. Every scientist who has seriously studied the Shroud has met with some version of this response. Instinctive disbelief is a common reaction.

The disbelieving view—the assumption that the Shroud *cannot possibly* be genuine—has its source in something other than scientific reasoning. It *is* hard to believe that the actual burial garment of Jesus Christ, imprinted with a detailed image of his body, possibly reposes today in a cathedral chapel in Turin, Italy. Yet archaeological artifacts, including burial clothes, survive from times earlier than the first century A.D., and there are things in the universe more curious than a mysterious image on a linen cloth. The likely reason for instant disbelief is that the Shroud may have something to do with Jesus Christ, along with the suggestion, seldom entirely absent in a discussion of the Shroud, that something miraculous is involved in its preservation and its image. In short, the Shroud seems to offend something in the modern temperament. It touches a nerve. Yet, mere disbelief does not deal realistically with the question of the Shroud's possible authenticity.

Some people are hostile to the Shroud. Madalyn Murray O'Hair, the noted American atheist, labeled the Shroud a fraud in a speech at Eastertime 1981. (Her speech was an attack on Jesus Christ and the church.) People who are hostile to the Shroud are often hostile to Christianity and to the man who is at the center of the Christian faith. Some single out the Shroud as an object of their emotional non-belief. The atheists' nonbelief mimics Christian faith, just as organized atheism mimics organized religion.

Many Christians view the Shroud with suspicion and are wary of talk about its possible significance. Many of these people are Protestants—both conservative and liberal—but others are Catholics. Their complaint is that the Shroud distracts Christians from more important elements in the Christian life—the Bible, fervent faith in God, service to others. These Christians have a point. Relics have not always strengthened Christian faith. Relics *have* distracted Christians from more important things, and they have been abused. However, the remedy is not to dispense with all relics, but to investigate their authenticity. The Shroud of Turin, the greatest relic in Christian history if authentic, can build faith. It could possibly reveal much about the details of Jesus' crucifixion and death—the Atonement, the sacrificial act that Christians believe brought about man's salvation.

At the other extreme are Christians who revere the Shroud. For some, it is more important than the Bible, correct doctrine, loving service, or any other aspect of Christian life. These Christians, like those who are suspicious of the Shroud, need to correctly integrate it into their Christianity, if, in fact, the Shroud is authentic. They may sense something about the significance of the Shroud, but they err when they make it an object of faith in itself.

The intensity of many of these reactions is in a sense understandable. The Shroud may be important. The stakes are high. The fact that the Shroud may involve Jesus Christ elicits emotional responses, but also makes it imperative not to reach conclusions swiftly or lightly. Any conclusion that the Shroud is genuine must be based on a convincing body of facts. Caution is also in order if it seems likely that the Shroud is authentic. If the Shroud really is the burial garment of Jesus, we must carefully consider how to fit it into the scheme of our Christian faith and life.

Yet these real scientific and pastoral problems do not fully explain the phenomenon of the Shroud. It has spiritual roots as well. The claim about the Shroud involves Jesus Christ, and his claims on us are great as well. The Shroud seems to suggest that he died the way the scriptures say he did. If so, he may have risen from the dead the way the scriptures say he did. If he rose, then he conquered death and lives still. He is God as he said he was, and he demands obedience from us now, just as he did when he walked the earth. Some believe that this is the chain of implication involved in the Shroud of Turin. No man or woman can follow these implications lightly or calmly. When we look at pictures of the Shroud, or think and talk about it, we are considering possible evidence for the truth of the Christian faith. Those are the claims which must be investigated.

Until this century, the Shroud of Turin has been almost exclusively an object of interest to Roman Catholics. Catholics have viewed it, written about it, studied it, venerated it, and protected it. In recent years, however, the Shroud has become an object of intense interest to many others as well, including evangelical Protestants and scientists. In fact, many of the scientists who have studied the Shroud have been agnostics, and there is a great deal of general public interest in the Shroud among nonbelievers as well as believers. Why this burgeoning interest in an object traditionally associated with the Catholic Church?

One reason has been changes in Roman Catholic piety. The old-style Catholic piety, which sometimes led to the attribution of miraculous and wonder-working powers to the Shroud and other relics, is becoming a less prominent feature of daily Catholic life. At the same time, evangelical Protestants have realized that the Shroud, if authentic, contains valuable information about Jesus Christ, and that its implications could potentially help the cause of evangelism in the modern world. Viewed properly, the Shroud can build faith, not misdirect it.

However, the main reason for the new interest in the Shroud is, ironically, the rise of science. Science may have shaken the beliefs of many Christians, but it has only deepened the mystery surrounding the Shroud of Turin. Instead of debunking the Shroud, the intensive scientific investigations during the 1970s made it even more intriguing. Public interest has increased as chemists, physicists, engineers, and technicians admit their bewilderment at the image and the process that formed it.

The skeptical world-view which often accompanies modern science has ironically created a climate conducive to serious interest among Christians in the religious value of the Shroud. The question of authenticity has become more important than ever before. In the Middle Ages, the Shroud of Turin was of value primarily for personal piety. The church encouraged Catholics to use it as a way of meditating on the passion and death of Jesus Christ, but it did not make official claims that the Shroud was really the burial garment of Jesus. By contrast, the Shroud today begins to look as if it could challenge unbelief by offering physical evidence for the death and resurrection of Jesus Christ. The skeptical modern mind is receptive to such evidence precisely because it is skeptical. For some, perhaps, it is the only type of evidence that would be convincing.

This is why the Shroud is potentially so important. This is an age characterized by widespread rejection of the supernatural and the miraculous. This skepticism has invaded even the church. Many modern persons—even theologians, scripture scholars, and pastors—have a skeptical view of the literal, physical resurrection of Jesus Christ. "Scientific reasoning" compels them to doubt that Jesus actually rose from the dead. Many of them understand the resurrection as a "spiritual" phenomenon—Jesus "rose" in the minds of his disciples, and he lives on today in the "memory" of his followers.

It is hard to imagine a more effective challenge to this "scientific"view than the Shroud. If the Shroud is authentic, it could be the burial cloth of Jesus Christ, imprinted with a detailed image of his dead body and displaying signs that his body was inexplicably removed from its burial cloth. Could it be that the Shroud is a sign from God for our time? In an age when science is making faith in the gospel difficult, science may be going as far as it possibly could to provide evidence for the gospel's validity.

But this is getting ahead of ourselves. We cannot reflect on the possible significance of the Shroud until we assess the evidence for its authenticity. This we will do in the following chapters. We will adopt a cautious, even skeptical, posture;

where facts are incomplete or hard to interpret, we will say so. Yet we will try to assess the facts about the Shroud and make judgments about their significance. A major goal will be to reach a verdict. Science and history cannot *prove* that the Shroud of Turin is the burial garment of Jesus Christ, but it may be possible to reach a likely conclusion—"beyond a reasonable doubt," to borrow the American legal term. Most scientific conclusions about complex phenomena are actually judgments of probability. Scientists gather facts, and then make theories to explain those facts. The theories themselves are not facts. When scientists say they have reached a conclusion, they usually mean that a certain theory is the most likely explanation for the observed facts. Our goal will be to reach a conclusion of this type concerning the known facts about the Shroud of Turin.

Like many who have studied the Shroud, the authors were initially skeptical of it. Stevenson first heard about it while a cadet at the U.S. Air Force Academy. He later returned to the Academy to teach on its faculty. Studies of the Shroud by his friends at the Academy persuaded him to examine the facts carefully and eventually drew him into the Shroud of Turin Research Project.

Habermas read a book about the Shroud in 1965. Although he was intrigued by the story, the then available facts did not convince him of the Shroud's authenticity. This skepticism began to change as results from the scientific testing in the 1970s became available. The 1978 scientific investigation in particular provided the decisive empirical data which convinced him of its authenticity and opened the door for future study of its significance.

We wrote this book to provide a serious but popular presentation of the scientific data about the Shroud, as well as carefully reasoned conclusions about its possible significance. The book is unique in several respects. It is the only book about the Shroud which incorporates the results of the scientific testing and analysis conducted since 1978 by the Shroud of Turin Research Project, including the photographs taken during the testing. Both the authors are associated with the team; Stevenson is a full member, and Habermas is a research consultant to it. In addition, the authors lay great stress on the possible significance of the Shroud for a deeper understanding of the Christian faith. We are intrigued by the fact that the Shroud, if authentic, would tend to confirm the validity of the Christian faith. It would also reveal much about the crucifixion and death of Jesus and possibly something about his resurrection.

Because the Shroud is an unusual object for scientific study, we must clearly understand the framework within which we will present and assess the facts. We will not assume that the Shroud is genuine, or in any way favor a miraculous explanation of its image. At the same time, we—and the reader—cannot prejudice our study by rejecting the miraculous *a priori*, assuming that supernatural events cannot occur. In other words, our treatment of this subject will be balanced. We will avoid both a pious approach, which interprets every fact as proof of the validity of the Shroud, and a skeptical approach, which refuses to view the evidence objectively. We intend to treat the available data fairly so that our conclusions rest firmly on the known facts.

To this end we would caution the reader to read carefully and to weigh the evidence accordingly. Do not allow skepticism about miracles or a distaste for relics to mislead you. View the evidence as impartially as possible so that you can reach whichever conclusion is best supported by the facts.

This book is divided into three major parts. Section One is chiefly concerned with the scientific data and other evidence regarding the Shroud. We begin with the question of whether the Shroud can be traced back to the first century A.D. (Chapter Two). We then proceed to a description of the dead man buried in the garment (Chapter Three). Chapter Four compares the Shroud with the relevant New Testament texts concerning the burial of Jesus. Finally, the last two chapters in this section present the results of the scientific investigation of the Shroud: Chapter Five discusses research prior to October, 1978; Chapter Six presents the results of the 1978 testing and the subsequent analysis.

Section Two draws factual conclusions based on the data in Section One. Chapter Seven discusses whether the Shroud could be a delusion, a forgery, or some other kind of fake. We then deal with the question of whether the Shroud is an authentic archaeological artifact (Chapter Eight). Then we move to the crucial question of whether the Shroud really wrapped the dead body of Jesus (Chapter Nine). Section Three discusses the significance of the facts about the Shroud and is based on the facts discussed earlier. Chapter Ten examines whether the Shroud provides insights into the physical causes of the death of Jesus. Then in Chapter Eleven we proceed to one of the most crucial issues—does the Shroud offer important scientific evidence for the resurrection of Jesus? Chapter Twelve briefly outlines the naturalism-supernaturalism debate, and we ask whether the Shroud offers any assistance in resolving it. Lastly, a concluding discussion draws together some final overall observations (Chapter Thirteen).

Both authors applied their different training and backgrounds to the Shroud question. Stevenson, an engineer, participated in the scientific investigation, including the testing in Turin in October, 1978, and he serves as the official spokesman and editor for the Shroud of Turin Research Project. (He edited the *Proceedings of the 1977 Research Conference of Research on the Shroud*, the most extensive testing done prior to 1978.) Therefore, Stevenson took major responsibility for the material on the scientific investigation.

Habermas is a professor of historical and philosophical apologetics, and he has two previous books on a historical investigation of the resurrection of Jesus. In this book he was primarily concerned with the conclusions drawn from the known facts about the Shroud and the significance of these facts.

It should be noted, however, that both authors have contributed to the entire volume and made it a cohesive unit. As a result of this interdisciplinary effort, it should reflect a tempering of scientific, historical, and philosophical interests and offer a comprehensive treatment of the Shroud.

TWO

The Shroud and History

THE COMPLEX HISTORY OF the Shroud of Turin poses a problem for historians. If Christ's burial cloth, imprinted with an image of his crucified body, had survived throughout the centuries, it would have been famous. The Shroud would be the most awesome relic in all of Christian history; one would expect its existence to be well documented.

This is not the case. There is little historical record of the existence of Jesus' burial shroud before the mid-fourteenth century. In fact, such a shroud is scarcely even mentioned in any ancient source before the sixth century. The gospels are relatively silent about it, and the few scattered references to Jesus' burial garment in church liturgies do not constitute absolute proof that the Shroud actually existed during those years. Moreover, very few of the early references that do exist mention the most astounding fact—the image on the Shroud. Why, skeptics understandably ask, would no one have reported such a significant detail? Those who question the Shroud's authenticity have long regarded this lack of a solid historical record as the weakest link in the argument.

The problem is compounded by the fact that the circumstances surrounding the Shroud's emergence as a historical object appear suspicious. The Shroud first became known around 1357 when it was exhibited in a small wooden church in the sleepy French provincial town of Lirey, a village about one hundred miles southeast of Paris. The Shroud's owner, Geoffrey de Charny, had been killed the year before by the English at the Battle of Poitiers. Impoverished by her husband's death, his widow, Jeanne de Vergy, hoped to attract pilgrims—and their monetary offerings—by exhibiting Jesus' burial garment in the local church. Crowds did gather—but only for a time. Bishop Henri of Poitiers, the local ordinary, quickly ordered the exhibition stopped, apparently doubting that a French noble family of modest means could have come into the possession of the true Shroud.

Jeanne de Vergy and other members of the de Charny family never explained how Geoffrey de Charny managed to come into possession of so fabulous a relic. Indeed, the question remains unanswered to this day (although, as we shall see, there is a plausible explanation). When exhibition of the Shroud resumed twenty-five years later, Bishop Pierre D'Arcis, Bishop Henri's successor, branded the Shroud a forgery and insisted that Pope Clement VII stop the display. Only later, when the Shroud came into the possession of the powerful House of Savoy, was it finally accepted as the true Shroud of Christ. But even then, acceptance came slowly. The Roman Catholic Church, in fact, has never claimed that the Shroud is genuine. Now, in the twentieth century, some scientists accept the Shroud's authenticity more readily than medieval Christians did.

Can the silence of the historical record be explained? Is there any evidence for the Shroud's existence prior to its appearance in Lirey? There is, in fact, a case to be made for the historical authenticity of the Shroud. It is partly a circumstantial case, one relying on probabilities and likelihood, and it still contains a few gaps. Nevertheless, it is a plausible theory. In addition, scientific investigation has revealed other strong evidence for a first-century origin for the Shroud of Turin.

Hints from Art History

Our historical inquiry can begin with the image of the face of the man buried in the Shroud. The face—bearded, long-haired, with Semitic features—closely resembles the standard artistic rendition of the face of Christ. One of the authors of this book (Stevenson) often travels with a three-dimensional mock-up of the face of the man in the Shroud, created with the assistance of computer-aided image analysis. People immediately recognize this as the face of Christ—precisely because it *is* the standard face of Jesus in art. It seems that everyone has seen it before. The Shroud face either reflects or has influenced the way most artists have portrayed Jesus for centuries.

Why is this so? Skeptics argue that the similarity betrays forgery: the forger, presumably working in the fourteenth century, painted the face according to the standard artists' rendition of the face of Christ at the time. But if the Shroud is more than 700 years old, the same similarity would then argue for its authenticity. If it existed before the fourteenth century, the Shroud may have influenced or even determined the standard portrayal of Christ in art.

A French biologist and artist named Paul Vignon was probably the first person to note the similarities between the Shroud face and artistic renderings of the face of Jesus. Later researchers, most notably Edward Wuenschel, Maurus Green, and most recently, the British historian Ian Wilson, have done an exhaustive comparison of the Shroud face with ancient images, particularly Byzantine icons.[1] They have developed evidence for what has become known as the "iconographic theory," the theory that the Shroud was known to artists as early as the sixth century, and that it inspired the conventional likeness of Christ.

These art detectives have been diligent. Vignon and Wuenschel thought they could find twenty "oddities" in Byzantine frescos, paintings, and mosaics which resembled peculiarities of the Shroud image. Wilson decided that fifteen of these are substantial enough to offer evidence in support of the theory.[2] A close study of the face of the Shroud image, for example, reveals a transverse streak across the forehead, a three-sided "square" between the brows, a "V" shape at the bridge of the nose, a raised right eyebrow, an enlarged left nostril, a transverse line across the throat, and two strands of hair at the top of the forehead. These appear in Byzantine icons. The most unusual of the markings, a combination rectangle and "V" at the bridge of the nose, was found in eighty percent of all the icons examined. Wilson found almost equally high percentages for all of the markings over a representative group of icons. This high frequency of similarities suggests a relationship between the Shroud face and Byzantine depictions of Jesus.

Why would a competent artist include these peculiarities in his art? The obvious answer is that, for some reason, he believed they belonged there. Wilson and others suggest that artists were copying one image, a holy likeness of Jesus that was revered as genuine, and hence definitive.

This image, if it existed, seems to have begun to influence Christian art around the sixth century A.D. The appearance of Christ in portraits shifted dramatically around this time. Before the sixth century, there was little similarity among pictures of Christ; the earliest portraits show him as a beardless, short-haired youth.[3] The gospels give no information about his appearance, and Jews, the earliest Christians, probably shunned portraits of the Lord because Jewish law prohibited religious images.

Around the sixth century, however, a conventional likeness of Jesus began to emerge. The majority of these representations display at least some of the telltale peculiarities which are also visible in the ethereal, mysterious, image of the face of the dead man on the Shroud of Turin. Christ is bearded, even fork-bearded like the man in the Shroud. Often his right eyebrow is raised, sometimes his left, as if the artist understood that an image produced by contact with his body would be reversed when viewed. Many of the Byzantine icons show a streak across the forehead and another across the throat, corresponding to fold marks on the Shroud face. Most of these icons have a peculiar box and "V" feature at the bridge of the nose. (See photos 1 and 2.)

How can this be explained? Did the Shroud image influence Christian art from the sixth century onward? If so, why doesn't history say more about the existence of Jesus' burial garment? This puzzle can help establish the existence of the Shroud of Turin before the mid-thirteenth century if there is a record of a holy image that was revered as the true likeness of Christ from the sixth century onward, and if that image was actually the Shroud in another guise.

The Mandylion

The reason for the shift in the artistic representation of Christ in the sixth century is no mystery. The image that changed Christian art is known to history. It was a representation of Christ's face known variously as the "image of Edessa," the "Edessan image," and the "Holy Mandylion." This was a cloth found in 525 A.D. in a niche above the west gate of the walls of the city of Edessa, now Urfa, in south central Turkey. In 944, the Mandylion was taken to Constantinople, the capital of the Eastern Empire, where it was revered as the true likeness of Christ. It was seldom exhibited publicly; an ancient Byzantine hymn suggests that it was regarded as too holy to be viewed. Yet monk-artists almost certainly saw it privately and used it as the model for the representation of Jesus on icons. Then in 1204, the Mandylion disappeared during the sack of Constantinople by a marauding mob of crusaders from Western Europe. Robert de Clari, a Crusader historian, inquired after the fate of the image and concluded that "neither Greek nor Frenchman knew what became of it."

The story of the origin of the holy image of Edessa is legendary; perhaps it contains a kernel of fact. It is said that Abgar V, first-century ruler of Edessa, was stricken with leprosy. He wrote to the healer-teacher Jesus of Nazareth in Palestine, asking him to come to Edessa to cure him. Jesus is said to have sent a letter declining to come, but promising to send a disciple instead. A disciple did eventually come after Jesus' death and resurrection, bearing with him a holy cloth imprinted with the Savior's image. At the sight of the cloth, Abgar was cured and the Christian faith was established in the city.[4]

Some accounts suggest that the disciple who brought the cloth to Edessa was Jude Thaddeus. If so, then the bearer of the Mandylion may have been close to the Lord, perhaps even a relative. Other scholars dispute the identification of Jude Thaddeus with the apostle Jude and identify the messenger to Edessa only as one of the seventy disciples.

There are some reliable historical facts behind this account. Abgar V really existed, and the Edessa area was evangelized soon after Jesus' departure from this world. There was a tradition in Edessa that a holy image of the Lord was associated with this evangelization.

The Holy Image of Edessa quickly disappeared from history. Abgar V's son, Man'nu, reverted to paganism and persecuted Edessa's Christians. The cloth vanished, but its memory was preserved, especially after Christianity was reestablished in Edessa around the end of the second century A.D.

Nearly 500 years later, in 525, a cloth bearing an image of Christ was found hidden in a niche above Edessa's west gate. Historians, particularly Ian Wilson, suggest that this cloth was the one associated with the reign of Abgar V. The Edessan Christians may have hidden the holy image in the city walls when Man'nu began to persecute them in the mid first century. They may have done this very quickly, perhaps under conditions of desperate danger, as Man'nu and his men hunted them down. Perhaps all those who knew the precise location of the holy cloth were killed, while the survivors preserved its memory.

If Christians hid the holy cloth, they could not have chosen a better hiding place. The niche in the wall was dark and protected from the elements, especially the severe floods which periodically devastated Edessa. It was rediscovered only because the walls themselves were being repaired. After its reappearance, the holy image was again revered and its discernible influence on art began at this time. The Emperor Justinian built a shrine and a cathedral for the cloth, and it somehow survived the frequent outbursts of iconoclasm in the eighth and ninth centuries during which many religious icons and paintings were destroyed.[5]

The holy image came to Constantinople in 944 as a result of what Wilson calls "one of the most bizarre military missions in all history." The aged and superstitious Byzantine Emperor, Romanus Lecapenus, decided to bring the Mandylion to Constantinople, the center of Eastern Orthodoxy. Romanus thought that this famous relic would provide divine protection for his city, and he was probably motivated by a desire to procure it from a city in Moslem territory. Romanus sent his most able general on a campaign across Asia Minor to retrieve the cloth. When the army reached Edessa, its commander offered the city's emir a strange but attractive deal. In return for the image, the army would spare Edessa, release 200 Moslem prisoners, pay a ransom, and guarantee Edessa's perpetual immunity from attack. The emir eventually agreed to these demands, but then Romanus' army had to contend with Edessa's outraged Christian minority, which, of course, revered the image and refused to surrender it. The Christians twice tried to pass off copies of the original, but eventually Romanus' men secured the real cloth and returned it in honor to Constantinople.[6]

In Constantinople, the cloth became known as the Mandylion, a name derived from an Arabic word meaning veil or handkerchief. There it remained, one of the holiest and most revered of Orthodoxy's relics, until its disappearance in 1204. During these centuries, the Mandylion exerted its influence on the typical Byzantine portrait of Jesus.

The Mandylion vanished in an orgy of pillage and looting. A European army, gathered in Constantinople to prepare for the Fourth Crusade, decided to attack fellow Christians instead of infidels. It was one of the most shameful episodes in Western history. The crusaders looted houses, palaces, and Orthodox churches. A Christian army, supposedly marching for the glory of God, had struck a mortal blow at one of the world's great Christian cities.

The Shroud and the Mandylion

Were the Shroud and the Holy Mandylion the same cloth? Although the evidence from art history suggests a close connection, the link is not obvious and many questions must be answered. The very first question is why the disciples of Jesus would have allowed their Lord's burial shroud to leave their possession.

We cannot know for sure, but it is likely that the disciples regarded Jesus' burial garment somewhat differently than we might do today. For Jewish Christians, the most important feature of such a garment would have been the fact that it was a burial cloth—an unclean thing according to Jewish law. Anyone who touched it was rendered ritually impure. In addition, Jewish law prohibited religious images; this image would have revealed the details of a grisly scourging, beating, and crucifixion—the punishment of a criminal. In short, Jesus' disciples had good reason not to talk much about his burial shroud; they could have hidden it away carefully.

It is also necessary to bridge the gap between the Mandylion's disappearance in 1204 and the mysterious appearance of the Shroud in France in 1357. Nothing definite is known of the Mandylion after the sack of Constantinople. Some historians of the Edessa image surmise that the cloth was taken to Europe along with other looted relics and was destroyed in the French Revolution. One crusader thought that the Venetian Doge sent it to Venice, but the ship sank with all on board. Robert de Clari, the chronicler of the Fourth Crusade, says that no one knows what became of the Holy Mandylion.

Ian Wilson proposes an intriguing theory to link the Mandylion with the Shroud. He suggests that from 1204 to the early 1300s, the Shroud-Mandylion was in the possession of one of the most exotic and mysterious groups in the medieval church—the Knights Templars.[7]

The Knights Templars were a religious order of knights founded about eighty years before the sack of Constantinople for the purpose of defending the crusader territories in the

Holy Land. The Templars attracted powerful friends and noble members because they combined the two great passions of the Middle Ages—religious fervor and martial prowess. The members of the order took vows of poverty, chastity, and absolute obedience, and their courage in battle was legendary. They vowed never to retreat under attack, and they defended crusader territories in the Holy Land with resourcefulness and great bravery. By the time of the sack of Constantinople, the Templars had grown very powerful. They built impregnable fortresses in the Holy Land and in Europe, and princes and nobles in those unsettled times often entrusted their valuables to the Templars for safekeeping. Among these valuables were many relics.

The Templars surely had the strength and the motive to safeguard a relic as fabulous as the Mandylion-Shroud. As one of the principal traders of relics from the Fourth Crusade, the Templars would have been in a position to acquire it, and their wealth would have protected them from the common temptation to sell relics for much needed cash. They would have been able to keep its location secret in their network of fortresses and castles. As pious and noble knights, they would also have honored it.

Did the Knights Templars in fact acquire the Mandylion-Shroud and keep it hidden for 150 years? There is some suggestion that they did. The evidence is circumstantial, even fragmentary. It is, in large part, an argument from historical silence—the weakest of all historical arguments. *If* the Shroud and the Mandylion are the same, and *if* the cloth lay hidden for 150 years in Europe or the Near East, the secretive Knights Templars were the one group that could have hidden it.

One suggestive piece of evidence emerges from the rumors during the thirteenth century about the Knights' secret initiation rites and worship services. Scholarly debates continue to this day about what actually went on at these secret gatherings. The Templars' enemies, of which there were many, accused them of such offenses as spitting on the cross, denying Christ, sodomy, and idol worship. Most scholars find these charges unjustified. The Templars were orthodox Christians who gave admirable service to the church. Nevertheless there may have been some customs in their initiation and worship services that others may have interpreted as idol worship.

The Templars were said to worship a mysterious "head" at their secret ceremonies. During their initiation, which usually took place near a model of the tomb of Christ, each new Templar was given a white mantle imprinted with a red cross symbolizing Christ's crucified body. According to Wilson, "a special ceremony was devised for initiated members of the order, whereby they were given a momentary glimpse of the supreme vision of God obtainable on earth, before which they prostrated themselves in adoration."[8]

Could this vision have been a glimpse of the Mandylion-Shroud? The strongest indication that it could have been comes from a painting discovered in 1951 in a Templar ruin in the village of Templecombe, England. (See photo 3.) The painting resembles Byzantine copies of the Mandylion and also conforms to some of the vague Templar descriptions of the "head" that played such an important role in their initiation and worship ceremonies.

This possible link between the Templars and the Mandylion is paralleled by a possible connection between the Templars and the Shroud. On October 13, 1307, King Philip the Fair of France, the most powerful enemy of the Templars, suppressed the order. He imprisoned its members and subjected them to inquisition and torture. On March 19, 1314, the leaders of the French Templars were led to a public scaffold before the Cathedral of Notre Dame in Paris and ordered to repeat their "confessions,"which, of course, had already been extracted under torture. The grand master of the French Templars, Jacques de Molay, and one of his fellow leaders, refused to recant. Instead, they defended the order and repented for confessing to lies about it under threat of torture and execution. King Philip promptly spirited these men to a small island in the River Seine and had them slowly burned to death. It is said that de Molay, as he died, called down God's judgment on King Philip and the pope, who had acquiesced in the persecution of the Templars. As it happened, both men died within the year.

De Molay's companion at the stake was the master of the Knights Templars in Normandy. His name was Geoffrey de Charnay. His name, of course, is virtually the same as that of the first known owner of the Shroud—Geoffrey de Charny of Lirey. Spelling of proper names in medieval times was inexact. Although it is not firmly established, it is quite possible that Geoffrey de Charnay, the Templar, was of the same family as Geoffrey de Charny, the man who mysteriously turned up with the Shroud in the mid-1350s.

This intriguing bit of historical research establishes a possible connection between the Holy Mandylion and the Shroud of Turin. The Mandylion is a historical object whose existence and whereabouts are known from 525 to 1204. The Shroud is known to have existed since about 1357. Artists who modeled their paintings of Jesus on the Mandylion image produced icons that uncannily resemble the face of the man in the Shroud. Were the Shroud and the Mandylion the same?

There is one strong objection to the Mandylion-Shroud connection. The Shroud is fourteen feet long, three-and-a-half feet wide, and bears an image of both the front and the back of a dead man. The Holy Image of Edessa, the Mandylion, was only a face. Indeed, as noted earlier, the word *mandylion* is derived from an Arabic word which meant a veil or a handkerchief. If the Mandylion was the Shroud, its true nature must have been disguised for many centuries.

Wilson suggests that the nature of the Mandylion was indeed disguised. Early in its history, he says, the Shroud was folded up in a "doubled-in-four" fashion so that only the face was displayed. Artisans then surrounded the face with an ornamental trellis and placed the cloth in a frame. Indeed, traces of trellis-work decoration are found in some Byzantine copies of the Mandylion. The folding and decoration could have disguised the true nature of the Shroud for a millennum, perhaps until some Templar knight in the early thirteenth century closely examined the holy relic from Constantinople and discovered to his astonishment what it really was.

Why would the Shroud have been disguised in this way? It has already been noted that most first-century Jews, even Christian Jews, would have regarded burial garments as unclean objects. Many would have been embarrassed, even horrified, at a bloodstained burial garment containing the signs of a brutal beating and grisly crucifixion. They may well have decided at an early stage to disguise the true nature of the cloth.

The Byzantine Christians seem to have shared some of this early Christian abhorrence toward Christ's suffering and crucifixion. Edward Wuenschel, one of the early Shroud historians, points out that realistic depictions of the crucifixion did not become common until the thirteenth century, and even then they remained a feature of the Christian West. By contrast, the Byzantine Greek artists either depicted Christ reigning in glory, or used a symbol such as a lamb to suggest his sacrificial atonement.[9] Wilson cites several historical references indicating that the Byzantines knew the true nature of the Mandylion— that it was a full-length burial shroud and not simply a face cloth.[10] If so, perhaps simple prudence dictated that they keep silent about this fact.

Physical inspection of the Shroud indicates that Wilson's "doubled-in-four" theory is likely. John Jackson, an Air Force physicist who was one of the organizers of the Shroud of Turin Research Project, reconstructed the pattern of the folds. Using Shroud photographs and a life-size mock-up of the cloth, he found that doubling the cloth in four did indeed expose the face area. Furthermore, Jackson found an eight-fold pattern of folds, visible in a new series of photographs of the Shroud, which is exactly consistent with Wilson's doubling in four. Jackson pointed out that these folds are rather inconspicuous when the Shroud is viewed. They may have escaped notice before because the human eye has trouble sorting out the faint, blurry body-image from other more prominent features of the cloth. Some of these other images are quite prominent and disconcerting, such as the fire damage and water marks. For many, viewing the image on the Shroud is similar to deciphering Rorschach diagrams or those business cards which cleverly disguise the face of Jesus in patterns of black and white. Among the images the eye rejects are the signs of the doubled-in-four folds. However, this configuration appears in photographs.

If only the face of the Shroud image was exposed for so many centuries, why are signs of this not more visible now that the cloth is stretched out? If the Shroud spent more than half its life as the Mandylion, there should be a circular area around the face of Christ which is more yellowed than the rest of the cloth. But perhaps the Mandylion was never exposed to the open air and sunlight often enough to become visibly discolored. If the Shroud and the Mandylion are indeed the same, then the Shroud was hermetically sealed in the Edessa city wall for 500 years, and later kept in a reliquary where it was removed only twice a year in Edessa and only once a year in Constantinople. Private showings of the Mandylion for dignitaries and artists would have been conducted indoors. So in the course of twelve centuries the cloth's actual exposure to heat, air, and sunlight may have amounted to only a few hundred days.[11]

There is also other evidence suggesting that the Mandylion and the Shroud were the same. As already noted, the Shroud image appears blurred and dim, especially when viewed closely. Descriptions of the Mandylion are similar. One Byzantine writer in the tenth century described the image as "a moist secretion without coloring or painter's art."[12] When the Mandylion first arrived in Constantinople, the sons of the Emperor Romanus were disappointed because they were unable to distinguish Christ's features clearly. Stories were told to explain how this holy but indistinct image was formed. The Byzantine Greeks thought that Christ had miraculously formed the image by drying his face with a cloth or by wiping his sweat-soaked face in the Garden of Gethsemane.

These stories are the source of the legend of Veronica's Veil. It is said that Veronica, a pious woman of Jerusalem, rushed into the street as Jesus was being led to Calvary. She offered Jesus her veil to wipe his sweat- and blood-soaked face. He did, and when he returned it she found that his image had been miraculously impressed on the cloth.[13] The very word "Veronica" suggests the source of the story: *Vera* means "true," and *icon* means "likeness." This was how the image of Edessa was described: it was "a true likeness," an image "not made by human hands."

The history of the Shroud is incomplete. It may never be known for certain whether the Shroud of Turin and the Holy Mandylion of Edessa and Constantinople are the same object. Yet the historical case that the two cloths are the same is a convincing one. Much of the data is subject to different interpretations in detail, but, taken together, the connection between the two is highly plausible—even probable.

Scientific Studies

Apart from the historical case, modern scientific inquiry has produced independent evidence that the Shroud dates from the first century A.D. Several scientific studies conducted within the last decade suggest that the Shroud was already an ancient object when it emerged into history in 1357.

In 1973, Max Frei, a Swiss criminologist, was asked to authenticate the photographs taken of the Shroud in 1969. Frei, a botanist by training, noticed pollen spores on the cloth and received permission to sample them. Over the next few months, Frei laboriously separated the different spores, photographed them, and matched them to their plants by reference to botanical texts and catalogues.

Frei identified spores from forty-nine different plants.[14] Some of these plants grow in Europe, hardly a surprise since the Shroud has often been exposed to the open air in France and Italy, and would have picked up local air-borne pollen spores. But thirty-three of these plants grow only in Palestine, the southern steppes of Turkey, or the area of Istanbul. The Shroud has never left Europe since its appearance in Lirey in 1357. Frei's meticulous work strongly indicates that the Shroud was exposed to the open air in Palestine and Turkey at some point in its history—just as Wilson's Mandylion-Shroud theory suggests. Frei indicated that the overlay of the pollen grains convinced him that the Shroud has a first-century origin, although this cannot be absolutely proven by the pollen analysis.

Two other studies also bear on the Shroud's pre-1357 existence. Gilbert Raes, a professor at the Ghent Institute of Textile Technology in Belgium, inspected some threads removed from the cloth by a scientific team in 1973. He concluded that the weave of the linen was a type common in the Middle East in the first century A.D. (See photo 5.) Raes also observed something very interesting: traces of cotton among the linen fibers. He thought the cloth had been woven on a loom also used for cotton. Cotton, of course, is grown throughout the Middle East, but not in Europe.[15] Raes' finding was supported by Silvio Curto, associate professor of Egyptology at the University of Turin and a member of the commission of Italian scientists who examined the Shroud in 1973. "The fabric of the Shroud," Curto said, "*can* date back to the time of Christ."[16] If the Shroud is a fraud, a European forger would have had to have gone to the enormous trouble of procuring a cloth from the Middle East for his work, one which contained microscopic traces of cotton in the weave and pollen spores from non-European plants. He would have had no motive to do this because the science of his age could not have determined the place of origin of the cloth. In addition, such an act would have ignored the age of the cloth.

The final study bearing on the Shroud's age is a result of the 1976 experiments showing that the Shroud has three-dimensional data encoded within it. (We will discuss this discovery in detail in Chapter Five.)

John Jackson and Eric Jumper, the physicists who discovered the three-dimensional image, noted objects placed over the eyes of the man buried in the Shroud. They suggested that these objects might be coins. If so, they said that the ancient coin which was of the same size as the "buttonlike" images was the lepton of Pontius Pilate, minted between 14 and 37 A.D.[17] Francis Filas, professor at Loyola University in Chicago, says that the images are indeed coins, and that the coins are leptons. He says that computer enhancement and analysis of the images reveals that the objects have twenty-four coincidences of dimensions, location, selection, order, and angles "fitting only a coin issued by Pontius Pilate between 29 and 32

A.D."[18] This lepton is decorated with an astrologer's staff and four Greek letters (see photos 6 and 7). Some Shroud experts are taking a wait-and-see attitude on this point, but Filas' evidence strongly indicates a first-century origin for the Shroud. Studies of remains in first-century Jewish cemeteries confirm that the Jews placed coins over the eyes of the dead.[19]

The Shroud has not been dated by means of the carbon-14 dating procedure, a process which estimates the age of organic material by estimating the rate of deterioration of the radioactive carbon-14 isotope. All living things contain a small amount of carbon-14. It begins to deteriorate at a known rate when the living thing dies. The Shroud is linen, a fabric made from flax. The carbon-14 in the flax began to decay when the flax was cut.

The carbon-14 test will probably be performed on the Shroud eventually. Improvements in the technique have made it possible to date small samples of material. However, there are still obstacles to the carbon-14 test of the Shroud. Carbon-14 dating is a destructive test. The Shroud's owner and custodians are understandably reluctant to allow even a small amount of the Shroud to be destroyed. Some scientists question whether the small-sample technique is as accurate as older methods which required the destruction of large amounts of material. Questions have also been raised about the ability of scientists to purify a sample well enough to date it accurately. However, most experts believe these obstacles will eventually be overcome.

Until an accurate carbon-14 test is performed, we must conclude that the Shroud probably has a first-century origin. This is the date suggested by the studies of the textile, the pollen, and the coins.

The Later History of the Shroud

The history of the Shroud since 1357 is well documented. As we have already noted, it was first exhibited by Jeanne de Vergy in an obvious attempt to keep her family from financial destitution. Geoffrey de Charny, her husband and the Shroud's owner, was killed in the Battle of Poitiers. Pilgrims streamed to

Lirey to see the cloth, but Bishop Henri of Poitiers ordered the exhibition stopped. None of the de Charny family ever explained how the Shroud came into its possession. The Templar connection could explain much of this mystery that surrounded the first historical appearance of the Shroud. Geoffrey de Charny may well have been a member of the family of the executed Templar leader Geoffrey de Charnay. Could de Charnay have whisked the Shroud into his family's safekeeping while knights at the order's Paris headquarters resisted Philip the Fair's suppression of the order in 1307? If de Charny of Lirey came into possession of the Shroud this way, he had good reason to be quiet about it. The Knights Templars had been accused of idol worship; was the Shroud the idol? As a devoted and courageous servant of the French king, de Charny would not have wanted to embroil himself in any revival of the king-Templar tragedy.

Bishop Pierre D'Arcis of Troyes, Henri's successor, was also skeptical of the Shroud when it was exhibited again in 1389. Jeanne de Vergy and her son, Geoffrey II de Charny, had carefully obtained permission to exhibit the Shroud directly from Pope Clement VII, bypassing Bishop D'Arcis. In his indignation, the bishop wrote a bitter letter to the pope, in the course of which he claimed that the Lirey Shroud was a known forgery. (The contents of this so-called "D'Arcis Memorandum" are discussed in detail later in Chapter Seven of this book.) Pope Clement rejected D'Arcis' protests and ordered him to keep perpetual silence on the matter under pain of excommunication. However, the pope also ratified an earlier decision that Jeanne and Geoffrey describe their cloth only as a "representation" of the true shroud.

In subsequent years, the de Charny family fell on hard times. Geoffrey II de Charny died in 1398, and his daughter and heir, Margaret de Charny, failed to produce an heir of her own. The wooden church at Lirey where the Shroud was kept began to fall into a state of disrepair. Toward the end of her life, Margaret de Charny, apparently convinced that the Shroud faced an uncertain future after her death, began to look for a suitable family to take possession of it. She settled on the House of

Savoy, a pious and powerful noble family which was expand-
ing its domains in the area of northern Italy, Switzerland, and
southeastern France. She deeded the Shroud to Louis of Savoy
in 1453, and the House of Savoy has owned it ever since.

Margaret de Charny made a wise choice. The House of
Savoy was successful in war and politics, and the head of the
family eventually became the king of Italy. The present legal
owner of the Shroud is not the Roman Catholic Church, as is
popularly believed, but the last king of Italy, Umberto II, who
lives in exile in Portugal. All exhibition and testing of the
Shroud require the permission of both King Umberto and the
Archbishop of Turin, its custodian.

Under Savoy patronage, the Shroud gradually gained a reputation as the true burial garment of Jesus. Around the year
1464, Pope Sixtus IV let it be known that he regarded it as an
authentic relic, and the dukes of Savoy built a special chapel
for it in the Savoy capital of Chambery, France. On December
4, 1532, fire broke out in the chapel and raged around the
silver-lined reliquary where the Shroud lay folded. The fire
melted part of the silver lining of the reliquary, and a piece of
molten silver fell on the folded cloth and burned it through.
One of the duke of Savoy's counselors and two Franciscan
priests carried the burning casket out of the building and doused
it with water, extinguishing the blaze. Happily the image was
virtually untouched, but the marks of the fire and water disfig-
ure the Shroud to this day. However, as we shall see later, the
fire in the Chambery chapel provides scientists with a built-in
experiment to test various theories for how the Shroud image
was formed.

In 1578, the Savoys moved the Shroud to their new capital in
Turin, Italy. The Shroud has remained there ever since, except
for a six-year period during World War II when it was safe-
guarded in a remote abbey in the mountains of southern Italy.

The last phase of the Shroud's history began to unfold in
Turin in 1898 when an Italian photographer named Secondo
Pia was permitted to photograph it during a rare public exhibi-
tion. To his astonishment, Pia discovered that the image on the
Shroud is actually a negative. Its dim and blurred features

sprang to life when "printed" on the film in Pia's camera. Scientists immediately recognized the significance of Pia's photographs. Many of them had assumed that the Shroud was a forgery like numerous relics of the Middle Ages. But why would a fourteenth-century forger have painted the image on the Shroud in a *negative* form? The concept of negativity was unknown until the invention of photography in the nineteenth century.

Secondo Pia's photographs initiated the series of increasingly detailed scientific studies which culminated in the 1978 investigation by the Shroud of Turin Research Project. Medical experts studied Pia's photographs and discovered that the image on the Shroud contains a degree of anatomical detail that far surpasses the medical knowledge of the fourteenth century. Scholars pointed out the remarkable consistency between what is known about Jesus' crucifixion and burial and what happened to the crucified and buried man in the Shroud. In 1976, a team of U.S. Air Force scientists made the remarkable discovery that the image on the Shroud has three-dimensional data encoded within it. With computer analysis, a three-dimensional replica of the image can be constructed.

It almost seems that the Shroud's deepest secrets lay hidden for 2,000 years until men invented scientific instruments sophisticated enough to detect them. Perhaps the age of sophisticated science is also the age which most needs to confront the man in the Shroud.

What happened to the man in the Shroud? What can be said about the body that the cloth once held? What evidence is there to link the Shroud with Jesus Christ? Let us begin our study of the Shroud by studying the image.

THREE

The Man Buried in the Shroud

GEOFFREY ASHE, A BRITISH author who has studied the Shroud, said, "The Shroud is explicable if it once enwrapped a human body to which something extraordinary happened. It is not explicable otherwise."[1]

This conclusion has been upheld time and time again by physicians and pathologists. The first of these medical men was Yves Delage, professor of comparative anatomy at the Sorbonne and a convinced agnostic. Delage was intrigued by the anatomical perfection of the image. In 1902, after a detailed study, he reported that the medical evidence convinced him that the man of the Shroud was none other than the historical Jesus Christ of the New Testament. Other physicians have reached the same conclusion throughout the years. For example, Robert Bucklin, deputy medical examiner of Los Angeles County, holds that the medical facts cited by Delage are still "beyond dispute."

Delage met a backlash of criticism when he made his report to the French Academy of Sciences. Many of Delage's colleagues were outraged and the academy refused to publish his findings.[2]

Considering this severe rebuff, Delage's only recorded response is quite temperate. He wrote to a fellow scientist that his conclusion represented "a bundle of imposing probabilities." He went on:

> A religious question has been needlessly injected into a problem which in itself is purely scientific, with the result that feelings have run high, and reason has been led astray. If, instead of Christ, there were a question of some person like a Sargon, an Achilles or one of the Pharaohs, no one would have thought of making any objection. . . . I have been faithful to the true spirit of science in treating this question, intent only on the truth, not concerned in the least whether it would affect the interests of any religious party. . . . I recognize Christ as a historical personage and I see no reason why anyone should be scandalized that there still exist material traces of his earthly life."[3]

Delage saw an image that so impressed him that he identified it with Jesus Christ, this in spite of his open and unchanged agnosticism and the obvious risk to his professional reputation. Just what did Delage and others see?

The image is that of a bearded male, approximately 5'11" in height. The cloth was apparently draped over his front, pulled over his head, and placed between his back and a flat surface, forming an image showing both the front and back of his body end-to-end. The man's estimated age is 30-35 years, and his estimated body weight is about 175 pounds. The man is well-built and muscular—a man accustomed to manual labor. A variety of markings on the body indicate that he died a brutal death; there are cuts and bruises and gashes, puncture wounds, and a swollen abdomen. Of particular interest is the fact that the wounds in their entirety exactly match the wounds Christ received as recorded in the gospels. More importantly for scientific purposes, all of the wounds are anatomically correct to a surprising level of detail. They include such medically accurate facts as a characteristic "halo" around bloodstains suggesting the separation of blood and serum; fleckings and rivulets true to blood flows in nature; and swelling of the abdomen that indicates asphyxiation, the usual cause of death in crucifixion. All of these medical facts, as well as others, were unknown in the fourteenth century. As we shall see, several aspects of the Shroud image depict the man in ways contrary to the artistic representations of Christ in the Middle Ages. In addition, the body shows evidence of death and rigor mortis, but no sign of decay.

When estimates of the height of the man of the Shroud were first made, some objected that he was too tall for the first-century period. However, archaeologists have recently reported that the mean height of adult males found in a first-century Jewish grave site was approximately 5'10".[4] Our modern idea that ancient men and women were much shorter than we are today is based in part on the inaccurate observation that suits of medieval armor in today's museums reflect the height of males of that time. The truth is that most surviving suits of armor belonged to young pages and not mature knights.

T. Dale Stewart of the Smithsonian Museum of Natural Sciences reports that the man of the Shroud's beard, hair, and facial features are consistent with a Jewish or Semitic racial grouping. He is definitely not of Greco-Roman culture. Several Shroud researchers cite ethnologist and former Harvard professor Carleton Coon, who states, "Whoever the individual represented may have been, he is of a physical type found in modern times among Shephardic Jews and noble Arabs."[5] Several Orthodox Jewish rabbis and scholars have told us that they agree that the man's beard and hair style are consistent with that of Jews of the first century.

One of the more curious features of the image is a long streak of hair which falls from the head to the shoulder blade on the dorsal image. (See photo 9.) This streak looks much like an unbound pigtail. Ian Wilson, the British historian, was the first to call attention to this detail. He calls it "the most strikingly Jewish feature" on the Shroud.[6] The German scholar Gressman and the French scholar Daniel-Rops have shown that it was a common fashion for Jewish men in Jesus' time to wear their hair caught at the back of the neck in a pigtail form.[7] Orthodox Jewish rabbis and scholars confirm this. This is one of many aspects of the Shroud image which contradict the traditional Christian idea of Jesus' appearance. A forger would probably not have known that Jesus may have worn his hair in a pigtail form, and he would scarcely have painted him this way in the fourteenth century.

Next we will examine the wounds in detail. (See photos 8 and 9.) Some of the most dramatic are the dumbbell-shaped markings which pepper the entire body except for the head, feet, and forearms. These wounds are numerous, and they vary in intensity from light contusions to severe punctures. They generally appear in sets of three or four. The size and shape of these wounds is identical with the tip of the Roman *flagrum*—a multi-thonged whip weighted at the tips with bits of bone or lead. (See photo 13.) This is precisely the instrument that John's gospel says was used on Jesus. Beatings with the *flagrum* were so savage that Roman law forbade its use on Roman citizens.

These scourge wounds show much significant detail. Close-ups of the scratches and cuts suggest that the scourge instrument was sharpened or had edges. Studies of the geometry of the pattern of wounds suggest that the beating was inflicted by two scourgers (or one who changed sides) since on the dorsal image the directions converge from left to right. The same studies indicate that one of the scourgers was taller than the other and more sadistic in his tendency to lash the legs. Changes in the angles of certain blood flows indicate that the man of the Shroud bled in two positions. Thus he may have been scourged bent over a scourging post.[8] There are between 90 and 120 scourge wounds on the body. Some say this is too many for Jesus to have received because Jewish law limited the number to forty. However, the Romans had no such limit when flogging Jews. Even if they had deferred to Jewish law in this instance, the three-pronged whip alone would account for about 120 wounds.

The scourge wounds in the shoulder region have been spread

and altered by two large areas of abrasion. This indicates that a heavy rough-hewn object chaffed the already damaged skin.[9] This is consistent with the known fact that crucifixion victims, Jesus included, were forced to carry the horizontal crossbeam to the place of execution. It was uncommon for a person to be both scourged and crucified, but this happened to both Jesus and the man of the Shroud.

The scourging the man in the Shroud received was very severe. It may have caused his death, or at least hastened it. Anthony Sava, an American physician, says that the concussive blows of a severe, repeated beating in the chest area may have caused internal hemorrhaging in the victim's chest cavity. The chest cavity would have gradually filled with bloody fluid, thus exerting pressure on the lungs, causing or hastening death by asphyxiation.[10] Sava's theory of chest hemorrhaging is disputed by other pathologists, but it rightly emphasizes the ferocity of the scourging. Scripture says that Jesus' death occurred earlier than most crucifixion victims'. His brutal scourging could certainly account for this.

The same bloody fluid which may have filled the chest cavity because of scourging would have settled into two layers, the heavier blood cells at the bottom and lighter serum at the top. If the chest cavity was pierced, the fluid would have flowed out in two forms—blood first, then the lighter serum. The Shroud image shows that the man of the Shroud was wounded in the side and a fluid leaked out which, especially on the dorsal image, separated into these two components.[11] (See photos 9 and 10.) Is this the blood and water outflow of John 19:34? The side wound is an oval shape that measures 1¾ inches by ⁷⁄₁₆ of an inch; it appears on the right side of the body between the fifth and sixth ribs. This wound exactly matches the shape of another Roman weapon, the *lancia*.

The knees of the man of the Shroud reveal cuts and bruises, particularly a large one at the left kneecap—an indication that the man fell. It has traditionally been believed that Jesus fell on his way to Golgotha, and that it was for this reason that Simon the Cyrene was pressed into service to carry the cross (Matthew 27:32; Mark 15:21; Luke 23:26).

Three of the wounds of crucifixion itself are clearly visible on the Shroud—the pierced left wrist on the frontal image and the two pierced feet on the dorsal image. (The right wrist is covered by the left hand, but the blood which flowed from it is clearly visible.) The feet were overlapped and a single spike was driven through both. This forces the weight down on one spot and yet still allows the legs to support the body. The hands were nailed to the crossbeam in such a way as to allow the body to take two positions on the cross. In the first, the weight is on the arms and the body slumps. This position forces the chest muscles to compress the lungs and makes breathing extremely difficult. The man of the Shroud had a build-up of fluid in the pleural cavity, making breathing even more difficult. In the second position, the legs raise the body in order to free pressure on the lung cavity to make it possible to breathe again.

The image shows blood flows from the wrist in two directions—consistent with two positions on the cross. (See photo 11.) The only place in the hand area capable of sustaining the body's weight and the necessary rocking or shifting back and forth is the wrist. Yet Christian tradition says that Jesus was nailed through the palms, and artists almost unanimously choose to depict the crucified Redeemer this way. Yet the anatomical facts, unknown to medieval artists, were that a body nailed through the hands would have ripped away from the cross.

In fact, the Bible does not say that Jesus was nailed through the palms. The Hebrew word *yad*, used in the messianic prophecy in Psalm 22:16 ("they have pierced my hands and feet"), was "used in a great variety of applications, and even included "armholes."[12] This certainly leaves sufficient margin to include the wrist area. Nor is the Greek of the New Testament any more precise. Jesus could have been nailed anywhere in the area of the hand and wrist and the beginning of the forearm.

A nail could be driven through the wrist in only one place without shattering the bones—a tiny spot between three bones called "the space of Destot." This opening was not described by anatomists until the nineteenth century. It also seems to have been known by executioners in ancient times. A nail driven into this opening will enlarge it and pass through without shattering bones. Surrounded by bone, the nail would give ample support to the weight of a body on the cross.[13]

A nail driven through the space of Destot will also sever or damage the median nerve which flexes the thumbs, causing the thumbs to draw tightly to the hand.[14] Thumbs are not visible on the Shroud image. Recent research with computer-enhanced photographs indicates that thumbs are present in the image but drawn tightly to the hand. What forger would have known about the space of Destot unless he was a first-century executioner or a nineteenth-century anatomist? How could he have known that a nail driven through the space of Destot would have severed the median nerve, causing the thumbs to curl tightly to the hand? Many anatomists who have studied the Shroud regard these facts as convincing evidence of its authenticity.

The image also reveals much about the man's death. All agree it was death by crucifixion, in essence a slow form of asphyxiation. The agony of the victims was publicly displayed both as a deterrent and as a grotesque thrill to the more macabre. Because crucified victims could survive for rather long periods of time if they were in good physical condition, executioners normally induced death in a particularly brutal way. When the signal was given, the executioner administered the *crucifragium*—a blow with a heavy mallet designed to break the legs. Victims then no longer had the ability to lock their knees or support their bodies on the legs; asphyxiation came quickly. The man of the Shroud, like Jesus, did not have his legs broken. There was no need. He was already dead, as his swollen abdomen clearly indicates.[15] Again, it is interesting to note that most paintings or sculptures of the crucifixion show Jesus with a sunken belly. Artists did not know the medical significance of a swollen abdomen, and therefore did not portray it in their paintings of the crucifixion.

The face of the man of the Shroud is covered with multiple bruises and swellings. (See photo 12.) The most noteworthy of these are a swelling which almost closes the right eye, and an abrasion coupled with possible separation of the nasal cartilage. The former indicates that the man was struck in the face; the latter might have been caused by an unimpeded fall with the weight of the crossbeam bearing him down. There is even evidence that part of his beard may have been plucked out, as gaps are apparent in front of it. Although this punishment is not recorded in the gospels, Jews inflicted it for the singular crime of blasphemy— the charge against Christ. It was specifically prophesied concerning the Messiah: "I gave my back to the smiters, and my cheeks to them that plucked off the hair: I hid not my face from shame and spitting" (Isaiah 50:6).

For many who have studied the image, the wounds that appear to identify the man as Jesus Christ most specifically are the numerous deep puncture wounds over the entire scalp. (See photo 26.) These could well have been caused by a covering of sharp thorns. In traditional Christian art, the crown of thorns was depicted as a circlet or a wreath. An occasional artist depicted the crown as a total covering, but such a style was rare before a time when the Shroud was already known. As Giulio Ricci points out, the crowning with thorns is virtually singular in history.[16]

The punishment inflicted on the man of the Shroud is identical, to an exacting level of anatomical and pathological accuracy, with that described in the gospel record of Jesus' passion and death. As Vignon wrote, "No painter, in his most elaborate work, has ever risen to such exactitude."[17]

Did an artist produce the image? Consider what a visual inspection of the image shows would have been required of this fourteenth-century genius. The artist would have had to have been one of the greatest who ever lived, a man capable of painting an image with the finest detail in a *negative* form. He would also have to know these medical facts many centuries before they were described by anatomists and pathologists: a severe chest beating can cause the pleural cavity to fill with a bloody fluid; this fluid would separate into two layers of heavy blood and lighter serum; a puncture through the fifth and sixth ribs would drain this cavity; a crucified man's abdomen would swell; the weight of a body can be supported on a cross if the arms are nailed through the space of Destot in the wrist; and this nail would likely sever the median nerve, causing the thumbs to cling tightly to the hand. This hypothetical artist would also have had to be daring enough to depart from Christian tradition in art by depicting Jesus nude, nailed through his wrists, wearing a cap of thorns covering the entire head, bearing approximately 120 scourge wounds, and wearing his hair in a pigtail. Finally, he would have to have had access to a Roman *flagrum* and *lancia* so that he could draw wounds that would exactly correspond to these archaeological artifacts. (We will consider the question of fraud in more detail in Chapter Seven.)

No wonder Yves Delage staked his professional reputation on the conclusion that the man of the Shroud is Jesus. He was convinced by the correlation of detail. The evidence is circumstantial of course, but Vignon, Barbet, Sava, Bucklin, and a host of other medical experts, believers and skeptics alike, have all reached the same conclusion. Meanwhile the amount of evidence continues to grow. A friend of ours, a scientist, has stated, "It would be more of a miracle if the Shroud were to be shown bogus than authentic."

FOUR

The New Testament
and the Shroud

THE IMAGE OF THE man of the Shroud contains much information about how the man died and was buried. How does it compare with what we know of Jesus' crucifixion and burial as recorded in the gospels? The question is important for both scientific and religious reasons. The gospels have been shown to be reliable sources; they tell us much of what we know today about Roman crucifixion practices and Jewish burial customs. If, as the image indicates, the man in the Shroud is a Jew crucified by the Romans, the circumstances of his death and burial should be consistent with what the gospels say about these things.

The religious reasons for this comparison should be obvious. If the Shroud is the actual burial garment of Jesus, then it should be consistent with the New Testament texts. This condition must be satisfied before anyone can identify the cloth as Jesus' burial garment.

Crucifixion

We have already mentioned some of the parallels between the man of the Shroud and Roman crucifixion practices. A closer look at these parallels reveals a remarkably close correlation. Let us compare relevant New Testament texts with details of the Shroud image.

Then Pilate took Jesus and scourged him. (John 19:1. See also Matthew 27:26; Mark 15:15.)

Approximately 120 scourge wounds can be observed on the body of the man of the Shroud. They were most likely inflicted by the Roman *flagrum*, a multi-pronged whip which was designed to rip out pieces of flesh with each blow. The scourging was so severe that some pathologists believe it was the primary cause of the man's death. It certainly hastened it.

They struck his head with a reed, and spat upon him. (Mark 15:19. See also Matthew 27:29; John 19:2.)

The face of the man of the Shroud is disfigured with bruises and swellings. The right eye is nearly swollen shut, and his nose is twisted. The man was almost certainly beaten in the face.

Plaiting a crown of thorns they put it on his head.(Matthew 27:29. See also Mark 15:17-20; John 19:2.)

The head of the man of the Shroud bled profusely from numerous puncture wounds in the scalp. These were probably caused by a cap of thorns which covered the top and sides of his head.

So they took Jesus, and he went out, bearing his own cross.(John 19:17.)

Bruises on the shoulders indicate that the man of the Shroud carried a heavy object. This had to have occurred *after* the scourging because the shoulder rubbing slightly altered the scourge wounds underneath.

And as they led him away, they seized one Simon of Cyrene, who was coming in from the country, and laid on him the cross, to carry it behind Jesus.(Luke 23:26. See also Matthew 27:32; Mark 15:21.)

The implication of the gospel account is that Jesus, weakened by the savage scourging, was not able to carry the crossbeam to the place of execution, as crucifixion victims were usually forced to do. It is quite possible that Jesus fell before his executioners seized Simon to carry the cross for him. The Shroud image shows cuts on both knees, especially the left knee, indicating a bad fall on a hard surface.

"Unless I see in his hands the print of the nails, and place my finger in the mark of the nails, and place my hand in his side, I will not believe."(John 20:25. See also Luke 24:39.)

These words reveal that Jesus had been nailed to the cross in crucifixion. The Shroud image likewise reveals that the man had been pierced through the wrists at the base of the palms, as well as through the feet. Medical experts have no doubt that the man of the Shroud was crucified, as Jesus was.

And Jesus uttered a loud cry, and breathed his last. (Mark 15:37. See also Matthew 27:50; Luke 23:46; John 19:30.)

The man of the Shroud is dead. His swollen abdomen indicates that he died by asphyxiation, the way crucified victims died.

But when [the soldiers] came to Jesus and saw that he was already dead, they did not break his legs. But one of the soldiers pierced his side with a spear, and at once there came out blood and water. (John 19:33-34.)

The legs of the man of the Shroud are not broken. The image also shows a wound in his side and a blood and water mixture flowing from it.

In summary, the man of the Shroud was crucified the way Jesus was. The comparison of the New Testament and the Shroud image lines up at every point.

The Burial

A comparison of the burial of the man of the Shroud with Jesus' burial is quite fascinating. The gospels contain more information about the way Jesus died than about how he was buried. The same is true for the Shroud image. A comparison of the two requires careful research, as well as an understanding of key words in New Testament Greek.

Jewish Burial Customs. The first point of comparison is the cloth itself. The gospels say that Jesus was buried in a cloth (or cloths); the Shroud of Turin appears to be a burial cloth which medical experts say once held a dead body. The image reveals a man lying on his back with his feet close together. His elbows protrude from his sides and his hands are crossed over the pelvic area. We can ascertain that the linen sheet was wound lengthwise up the front and down the back of the corpse. (See photo 14.)

Is this kind of burial compatible with the New Testament reports? It is at least compatible with Jewish customs as we know them from extra-biblical sources. Recent archaeological excavations at the Qumran community found that the Essenes buried their dead in the way represented on the Shroud. Several skeletons were found lying on their backs, faces pointing upward, elbows bent outward, and their hands covering the pelvic region.[1] The protruding elbows rule out an Egyptian-type mummified burial.

Also very instructive is the *Code of Jewish Law*, which discusses burial procedures in its "Laws of Mourning." It instructs that a person executed by the government was to be buried in a single sheet.[2] This is another parallel with the Shroud.

Although the New Testament's description of typical first-century Jewish burial customs is not overly detailed, it does give the general features. The body was washed (Acts 9:37) and the hands and feet were bound (John 11:44). A cloth handkerchief (Greek, *sudarion*) was placed "around" the face (John 11:44; 20:7). The body was then wrapped in clean linen, often mixed with spices (John 19:39-40), and laid in the tomb or grave. The *Code of Jewish Law* adds that the Jews usually shaved the head and beard completely and cut the fingernails before burial.[3]

However, the gospels tell us that Jesus' burial was incomplete. Because the Sabbath was about to begin, he was removed from the cross and laid in the tomb rather hurriedly. This is why the women returned to the tomb on Sunday morning. They had prepared spices and ointments for Jesus' body, and they went to the tomb to apply them (Luke 23:54-56). It is not often noticed why the women went to the tomb. They certainly did not expect Jesus to rise (Luke 24:3-4; John 20:12-15). Rather they came in order to finish anointing Jesus' body with the prepared spices (Luke 24:1; Mark 16:1). They were worried about who would help them to move the stone from the entrance of the tomb so that they could finish the job begun before the Sabbath (Mark 16:3).

The gospels do not say to what extent the burial had been left unfinished. The New Testament says that Jesus was wrapped in linen with spices and a handkerchief after the custom of the Jews (John 19:40), but it does not say that his body was washed. At least to some degree, the anointing with spices was incomplete because the women returned to the tomb to complete the process. The scripture does not state specifically what other parts of the burial process were unfinished, if any.

Although apparently a Jew, it appears to some that the man of the Shroud was not buried in accordance with the complete ritual of Jewish burial. He was laid in a shroud, as Jews were, but his body was unwashed. Stains of what looks like blood are visible on the body image and on the cloth itself. Neither was his hair trimmed. Despite what looks like a hurried burial, he was wrapped in a shroud of good linen. However, the wrapping in linen is consistent with first-century Jewish custom.

The Wrapping. It is quite difficult to determine from the gospels the precise method used to wrap Jesus' body in the cloth since the four evangelists use several different Greek verbs to describe the process. Mark 15:46 states that Jesus was wrapped (*eneilesen*) in a linen sheet. Matthew 27:59 and Luke 23:53 describe the body as being wrapped, or folded (*enetylixen*) in the linen cloth. John 19:40 says that Jesus was bound (*edesan*) in linen clothes. These Greek words are similar, yet they do not reveal the exact method utilized.[4]

McDowell and some others detect a problem in John's word

to describe the "binding" of the body.[5] They suggest that Jesus' body was wrapped tightly like an Egyptian mummy, a procedure which would not have yielded an image such as the one on the Shroud. However, the mummy idea largely rests on variant readings in the extant manuscripts of John's Gospel. One late manuscript uses a verb in 19:40 which suggests a tight binding of the body. The accepted verb, however, is *edesan*, a verb which means to "wrap" or "fold" and which is quite compatible with the synoptic verbs. The idea that Jesus was tightly bound like a mummy is also incompatible with John's earlier description of the way Lazarus emerged from the tomb after Jesus raised him from the dead (John 11:44). Lazarus, who was buried according to Jewish custom, was able to proceed from the tomb by his own power, although he was impaired and had to be "unbound." He had his hands and feet bound, as was the custom, but he was not completely wrapped up.[6]

In other words, the type of wrapping depicted in the Shroud is compatible with Jewish burial technique. In particular, the burial methods depicted both in the Essene cemetery and described in the *Code of Jewish Law* favor the Shroud. Along with the Lazarus account, these sources convince us that the type of wrapping demanded by the Shroud was at least practiced in Israel in Jesus' time, and may even have been the most popular practice. At any rate, it cannot be asserted that Jesus must have been buried as a mummy.

The Grave Clothes. Another issue concerns the difference in the words chosen by the gospel writers to describe the grave clothes that Jesus was wrapped in.[7] The synoptic evangelists say that he was wrapped in a *sindon*, a Greek word meaning a linen cloth which could be used for any purpose, including burial. John, on the other hand, says Jesus was wrapped in *othonia*, a plural Greek word of uncertain meaning. *Othonia* is sometimes translated as "strips of linen," a meaning that would seem to be incompatible with a fourteen-foot-long shroud covering the front and back of the body. However, it is likely that *othonia* refers to *all* the grave clothes associated with Jesus' burial—the large *sindon* (the shroud), as well as the smaller strips of linen that bound the jaw, the hands, and the feet. This interpretation of *othonia* is supported by Luke's use of the word. He says (23:53) that Jesus was wrapped in a *sindon*, but later (24:12) that Peter saw the *othonia* lying in the tomb after Jesus' resurrection. Luke, then, uses *othonia* as a plural term for all the grave clothes, including the *sindon*.

Furthermore, as seen earlier, Jewish burial customs do not support the idea that John's *othonia* refers to the wrappings of a mummy. Jews did not wrap up their dead like mummies, but laid them in shrouds, as indicated by the Gospel of John, the Essene burial procedures, and the *Code of Jewish Law*. John himself insists that Jewish customs were followed Jesus' case (19:40). Thus, there is good scriptural evidence that Jesus was laid in the tomb wrapped in a shroud.

Therefore, the gospels refer to the grave clothes in both the singular and the plural. When a single cloth is spoken of, it is obviously the linen sheet itself. However, since Luke (or early tradition) had no difficulty in using the plural (24:12) to describe what he earlier referred to in the singular (23:53), the term "clothes" may still refer to a single piece of material. On the other hand, if more than one piece is meant, "clothes" is most probably a reference to both the sheet and the additional strips which were bound around the head, wrists, and feet, as indicated in John 11:44 (cf. John 19:40). Interestingly enough, bands in these same locations can be discerned on the Shroud of Turin. At any rate, it is a reasonable conclusion that at least one major linen sheet is being referred to in the gospels.

Another apparent problem crops up in the descriptions of the grave clothes the disciples saw in the tomb on Easter morning. Both Luke and John describe grave clothes in the tomb. Luke says that Peter went inside the tomb and saw the *othonia*—the generic term for all the grave clothes, including the shroud and the smaller pieces used to bind the jaw, hands, and feet. John, however, gives a more detailed description of what he and Peter saw, and he introduces another term into the grave clothes listing. When they went into the tomb, they saw the *othonia* lying on the ground, but also the *sudarion* lying rolled up in a place by itself, apart from these *othonia*. John adds the detail that the *sudarion* had been "around the head" of Jesus.

Sudarion means "napkin" or "sweat cloth." It is, at any rate, a rather small piece of cloth. If it had been placed over the face of Jesus in the tomb, no image of Jesus' face would have appeared on the Shroud. Since the Shroud of Turin bears the image of a face, the reference to a *sudarion* seems to challenge the authenticity of the Shroud. Indeed, some Christians have pointed to this passage as evidence that the Shroud is incompatible with scripture.

However, a number of scripture scholars do not think that the *sudarion* was a napkin or cloth placed over Jesus' face. The Mishnah instructs Jews to tie up the chin of the corpse (Shabbath 23:5). The *Code of Jewish Law* also commands the practice of binding the chin.[8] Lazarus' napkin was wrapped "around" his face (Greek, *perideo*), a position that is more consistent with the jaw being tied shut. Additionally, John's observation that Jesus' napkin was found "rolled up" (Greek, *entulisso*) in the empty tomb corresponds closely to the cloth being used to bind the jaw.[9]

John A.T. Robinson, the British New Testament scholar, gives the most plausible explanation for the *sudarion*. He says it was probably a jaw band, a piece of linen rolled up into a strip, placed under the chin, drawn up around the face, and tied on the top of the head. Its function was to keep the jaw shut before rigor mortis set in. Not only does the New Testament not state that the napkin was placed over the face so as to cover it, but the combination of "wrapped up" and "around the head" (John 20:7; cf. 11:44) fits what is depicted in the Shroud.

Jaw bands are used for this purpose today and there is every reason to believe that they were used in first-century Palestine. There is evidence for just such a jaw band on the three-dimensional image of the face of the Shroud. The hair of the man seems to be separated from the cheeks. The hair on the left side of the face hangs out over the edge of an object, probably the chin band.[10]

Why did the Gospel of John include this detail about the

sudarion? The author seems to attach great importance to it. He describes the burial cloth on the ground and the *sudarion* rolled up in a place by itself, and then adds that this discovery caused belief.

It is not easy to tell from the Greek exactly what it was about the placement of the grave clothes that caused belief (John 20:9), but Robinson has a plausible interpretation of what is being described here. We are told that the disciples entered the tomb and saw the shroud and the other linen cloths lying flat. But the *sudarion* was apparently still in its twisted oval shape, the way it had been when tied tightly around Jesus' head to keep the jaw closed. Something about this scene convinced them that grave robbers could not have stolen the body, as Mary Magdalene had reported after she discovered that the stone had been moved away from the tomb. Until this moment, the gospel explains, the disciples had not understood that Jesus would rise from the dead. Now, looking at the grave clothes, they believed.

The Unwashed Body. Another issue in the Shroud-New Testament correspondence, one already mentioned briefly, is Jesus' unwashed body. Since the Shroud unquestionably depicts an unwashed body, we should determine whether the New Testament says anything about this crucial fact. The Jews washed the bodies of their dead before burial, as people in most cultures do. However, the gospels do not say specifically that Jesus' body was washed. There is good reason to think it was not.

The gospels say that the coming of the Sabbath curtailed some of the activities involved in Jesus' burial (Luke 23:54-56). The Mishnah allows for the anointing and washing of a body on the Sabbath, but only if not a single portion of the body was moved (Shab 23:5). In other words, the body could have been washed, but not wrapped in a shroud and laid in the tomb. Therefore, if the whole burial process could not have been completed by the beginning of the Sabbath, there was sufficient reason to leave the body unwashed. We should remember here that the women returned to anoint the body with their prepared spices (Luke 24:1; Mark 16:1), which were used for several purposes, including cleansing. Since the gospels do not record the washing, it might be inferred that this was not done, but was left for the women after the Sabbath.[11]

Again the *Code of Jewish Law* assists us. The law relates that while washing and cutting of the hair and fingernails was the normal procedure in Jewish burial practice, these acts were not performed on persons who were executed by the government or the state, or those who died a violent death.[12] Since both these exceptions apply to Jesus, the washing of his body would have been prohibited on two counts.

There is one other suggestion that Jesus' body was not washed. This is John's statement that Jesus' body was wrapped in a large quantity of spices before burial (19:39-40). Since the women were returning to the tomb on Sunday in order to anoint the body with spices, what was the difference between the first anointing and the second?

The most likely explanation is that the large quantity of spices had been packed around Jesus' body before the burial precisely because the body had not been washed. This large quantity of spices, possibly in dry form, could have been intended to serve as a disinfectant to arrest decomposition until the women could properly anoint the body after the Sabbath. The spices which the women were bringing with them on Easter morning would probably have been applied during or after they washed the body. As it turned out, however, the temporary packing with spices just before burial was the only anointing Jesus' body received. Again, the New Testament does not indicate exactly how the spices were distributed, and there is no contradiction between the Shroud and the gospels. In fact, there is no contradiction between the gospels and the Shroud on any point.

One other issue might be quickly mentioned again. The gospels relate that Jesus' hands were nailed to the cross (Luke 24:39; John 20:20, 25-27) while the man of the Shroud was nailed through the wrists. There is no discrepancy here, for at least two reasons. First, the Greek word for "hand" can also refer to the wrist, thereby including both with the same word.

Second, the man of the Shroud was nailed at the base of the palm, in an area that could be described as either "hand" or "wrist." Even apart from the Shroud, scholars have long believed that crucifixion victims (including Jesus) were nailed through the upper wrist, since the palms would not normally sustain the weight of the human body. (See Chapter Ten.)

Conclusion

What can we conclude from this comparison of the Shroud with the New Testament texts? The first conclusion is a historical one. The burial received by the man in the Shroud is compatible with first-century Jewish burial customs as we know them from the New Testament, the *Code of Jewish Law*, and the Essene archaeological find. All these sources indicate that dead Jews in the first century were not bound up like mummies but were laid in tombs wrapped in a shroud. This was the way the man of the Shroud was buried. This is a very general conclusion. We cannot absolutely assert that burial like that seen in the case of the man of the Shroud was the universal custom in first-century Palestine. However, this study does suggest that wrapping in a shroud was a likely procedure. The Mishnah, the *Code of Jewish Law*, the Essene burial customs, and especially the New Testament texts such as John 11:44 and 20:7 show that the burial method used in the case of the man of the Shroud was, at the very least, a viable option known to be used by Jews in the first century.

Second, we can conclude that the burial of the man of the Shroud closely resembled that of the first century Jew about whose burial we know the most—Jesus Christ. Some of the burial rituals prescribed in Jewish law were not completed in his case and subsequent events prevented them from being completed after his entombment. As was probably true in Jesus' case, the body of the man of the Shroud was not washed.

We can draw a third conclusion which is relevant to the question of whether the man of the Shroud *is* Jesus Christ. Nothing in the New Testament rules out the possibility that the man is Jesus. This conclusion is possible because the New

Testament describes the general Jewish burial customs of the first century, but it does not describe the exact procedures used in Jesus' case. The exegetical study here cannot prove that the man is Jesus, but it cannot be concluded that he is Jesus if the Shroud image differs in any significant way from what the New Testament says about how Jesus was crucified and buried. The Shroud meets this test. The man of the Shroud was crucified the way Jesus was, and a close study of the texts reveals no incompatibility with the New Testament description of his burial.

Another point is worth making here. Something like the Shroud of Turin is not what one would expect a medieval forger to paint if he intended, as he certainly would, to base his artistry on the gospel descriptions of Jesus' burial. He probably would have painted a face cloth—the most obvious meaning of John's ambiguous *sudarion* in 20:7. He may have painted a washed body, because Acts 9:37 notes that the Christians washed Tabitha's body before they laid her out. He might even have painted a mummy. Bishop John A.T. Robinson says that his natural predisposition to skepticism about the Shroud was shaken precisely because "it could not at all easily be harmonized with the New Testament account of the grave clothes."[13]

Nevertheless, the issue of the authenticity of the Shroud must be finally settled on other grounds such as scientific testing. The Shroud of Turin is compatible with the New Testament texts and favored by important Jewish writings and customs. If rigorous scientific tests validate it, we will have a strong case for its authenticity.

FIVE

Science and the Shroud: Pre-1978

WHEN WORD LEAKED OUT that forty scientists from the Shroud of Turin Research Project were locked in a room with the Shroud of Turin, a syndicated cartoon captured some of the irony of the event. The drawing depicted a group of white-coated scientists in a laboratory examining the Shroud with space-age equipment. As they did, the image of the cloth quoted the scripture, "Blessed are they who have not seen and yet believe" (John 20:29). The drawing was not entirely fair, but it had a point. Many people, Catholics and evangelicals alike, viewed the research effort as a presumptuous attempt by science to probe mysteries best left to the realm of faith.

Yet the Shroud of Turin is not in itself an object of Christian belief, and scientists who study it are not implying that faith is subordinate to reason. The Shroud would still have religious value no matter what the scientists discovered about it. Indeed, the Shroud has been the object of scientific scrutiny for more than eighty years. Despite these studies, the scientists who have examined the image have for the most part managed to keep their science and their faith separate.

Early Studies: 1898 to 1969

The Shroud of Turin was a relatively obscure relic before 1898. Despite its exalted status as the reputed burial garment of the Redeemer, few of the miraculous healings and other notoriety that surrounded other famous relics were associated with it. The Shroud was publicly exhibited only five times during the nineteenth century. It was during the last of these expositions, held in 1898 to honor the Italian kingdom's fiftieth anniversary, that the new science of photography dramatically put an end to the Shroud's obscurity.

When the exposition drew to a close in May, 1898, a local lawyer named Secondo Pia was allowed to take the first photographs of the Shroud. His equipment failed on the first attempt, but Pia made good exposures on May 28. That night, in Pia's darkroom, one of the abiding secrets of the Shroud was first revealed. Pia removed his glass negative from the developing solution and discovered that the negative which he held in his hands was actually a "positive"—a "print" which was far more lifelike than the image viewed with the naked eye. This meant that the image on the Shroud was a negative. When printed, the dark areas of the image appeared light and the light areas appeared dark, and there was a left-right reversal of details. The result was a bold, detailed picture with striking contrasts, far more interesting than the soft, ethereal, dim image of the Shroud itself.[1]

Secondo Pia's remarkable photographs made the Shroud famous. They also made it an object of serious scientific study for the first time. The pictures revealed the corpse wrapped in the Shroud in excruciating detail. Forensic pathologists and other medical experts who examined the minutely detailed photographs were able to determine much about the sufferings which caused the man's death. For example, scientists could distinguish individual scratch marks within the "scourge wounds" on the dorsal image, and they could determine with a high degree of confidence that the man in the Shroud had been whipped by two men working on opposite sides of his back. (A description of the man in the Shroud is contained in Chapter Three.)

The most important scientific implication of Pia's discovery was that the Shroud was not an obvious forgery. Why would a fourteenth-century forger have painted a *negative* image? Not until the nineteenth century did anyone understand the concept of negativity: an image resembling the original would be created if light was projected onto a light-sensitive paper through a film in which the light-dark values were reversed. It seemed improbable that anyone would have known this in the fourteenth century. It was almost ludicrous to suggest that a painter, depicting Jesus' body as it might have appeared on his burial garment, would have chosen to do so with an artistry and detail that would have not been discovered for more than 500 years, until the invention of a photographic process which his age knew nothing about.

Scientists who considered the implications of Secondo Pia's photographs soon identified a key question: how was the image formed? At the turn of the century, Paul Vignon, a French biologist and artist, conducted a series of experiments to discover the process by which the image came to be printed on the cloth. Vignon's experiments convinced him that the image could not be a painting. He used conventional oil pigments and water colors to paint pictures on pieces of old linen; when he rolled up the cloth, as the Shroud was rolled, the dry pigment cracked and fell off. Vignon also considered the possiblity that a very light dye had been diffused into the fibers of the cloth. But such an image would not have been subject to a chemical process over the years which would have reversed the light and dark values—the only plausible way a negative image could have been produced.

Vignon then proposed a way in which he thought the image could have been printed on the cloth. He thought that the corpse somehow "projected"an image of itself onto the cloth. In a creative bit of theorizing, Vignon developed a hypothesis for how this could have happened. He speculated that the Shroud might have been treated with a mixture of myrrh and aloes—spices associated with Jewish burial—in a solution of olive oil. If so, the cloth would turn brown under the influence of alkaline vapors. Jesus' body (or the body of any crucified man) might have diffused just such vapors. The sweat produced in his death agony would have contained a high level of urea. Urea becomes a carbonate of ammonia when it ferments, and ammonia carbonate would stain the spice and olive oil-treated Shroud. Vignon never managed to duplicate this process experimentally in a laboratory, but his "vaporgraph theory" became a leading theory of image formation.[2]

In 1931, the Shroud was exhibited again, and new and better photographs were taken by Guiseppe Enrie, the leading photographer in Italy. These photographs made possible further scientific work. Some of the photographs were detailed enlargements: they showed no signs of pigment on the Shroud. On the basis of the photographs, textile experts classified the cloth as a type possibly common in Palestine in Jesus' time, but probably not in existence in Europe in the fourteenth-century. This meant that a forger in fourteenth-century France would very possibly have had to go to the trouble of obtaining a piece of ancient linen from the Holy Land for his master work in an age that could not tell the difference.

The Enrie photographs made possible the detailed study of the sufferings and wounds of the man in the Shroud. The most famous of these studies was made by Dr. Pierre Barbet, an eminent French surgeon, and author of the book, *A Doctor at Calvary*.

The Enrie photographs are the ones which everyone has seen; they were not surpassed in quality until the photographs taken by the Shroud of Turin Research Project in 1978.

More scientific data about the Shroud came from an unexpected quarter in 1968. Workmen excavating for an apartment block in Jerusalem uncovered the remains of a Jew who had been crucified by the Romans in the aftermath of the Great Revolt in 70 A.D. The archaeologists found the man's name written on his tomb—Yohanan. The work of the Israeli archaeologists who studied the skeleton allowed the Shroud researchers to conclude that the man in the Shroud had been executed in general accordance with the Roman practice of crucifixion. The Yohanan studies are summarized in Chapter Eight.

The 1969 Secret Commission

After a 1933 exposition, the Shroud was locked up in its reliquary for thirty-six years. Apart from six years of safekeeping in the mountains of southern Italy during World War II, the relic was kept in its locked and guarded vault in a chapel of the cathedral in Turin, unseen by the public or by scientists. Church authorities in Turin, entrusted with the task of safeguarding Christendom's most famous relic, long resisted pressure from scientists for direct testing and inspection of the cloth. To many, the Church's cautious and sometimes evasive attitude seemed motivated by a fear that scientists would prove that the Shroud was a fake. Perhaps, but the church's caution had other sources as well. The Shroud, after all, is primarily a religious object, revered by millions. Even if the Shroud is a fake, it still has religious value for some because it depicts in graphic detail the tortures inflicted on Jesus and the death he suffered to atone for mankind's sins. Scientists and journalists could not be expected to readily appreciate this point.

Some of the authorities also seemed to be indifferent to the Shroud and preoccupied with more pressing pastoral concerns. Cardinal Michele Pellegrino of Turin did not even view the cloth until 1969, many years after he took over his post as the Shroud's chief custodian. Pressure from influential Roman Catholic priests seems to have eventually succeeded in changing the church's resistence to scientific testing of the Shroud. The best-known of these men is Fr. Peter Rinaldi, an Italian-born priest who spent many years in the United States. He and others argued that if the Shroud was authentic, the Catholic Church should not keep an object of such enormous potential significance hidden away. It was worth the risk to determine the Shroud's authenticity once and for all.

These arguments had some effect. In 1969, Cardinal Pellegrino appointed a commission of ten men and one woman, including five scientists, to inspect the Shroud. Their instructions were to make proposals for future scientific study, and to determine if any special measures had to be taken to preserve the Shroud from deterioration in a modern industrial city with growing levels of air pollution. The commission was not able to accomplish much scientific work during the 1969 inspection. Many members of the commission had not studied the Shroud before and knew little about it. The commission did determine that the Shroud was in an excellent state of preservation. Beyond that, the members of the commission seem to have done little more than look at the Shroud and discuss it. The commission worked in secret, and its report was not released until 1976. By then, a far more significant series of studies had already been conducted.[3]

The 1973 Studies

Cardinal Pellegrino and the Shroud's owner, the exiled king of Italy, approved a television exposition of the Shroud in 1973. They also approved proposals from scientists to remove some threads from the cloth for analysis and to conduct other scientific tests. The scientific team which coordinated analysis of the Shroud was not well organized and its conclusions were regarded as disappointing by many. Nevertheless, the panel made some interesting discoveries and laid the groundwork for the more thorough and definitive testing eventually conducted in 1978.

One of the most interesting of the 1973 conclusions concerned the nature of the image on the Shroud. The Italian scientists found no pigment or dye in the image areas. Their inspection of the image under a microscope also revealed that it was superficial—that is, it lay on the very topmost fibers of the threads of the Shroud. They described the image as being composed of "yellow fibrils." The yellow color did not soak into or penetrate the fibers as a pigment or dye applied by an artist would have done. This observation also seemed to rule out Vignon's vaporgraph: the ammonia-soaked sweat diffusing from the body would have penetrated the fibers of the cloth, just like a pigment or a dye.

Analyzing these observations, Ray Rogers, an American chemist employed at the Los Alamos National Laboratory, suggested that the fire which burned part of the Shroud in 1532 supplied a ready-made experiment to assess various theories of how the image was formed. He pointed out that there was a large variation of heat intensity during the fire; some parts of the Shroud were burned, scorched, and severely discolored by the blaze, while other parts of the cloth were hardly affected at all. Rogers said that if any organic molecules, applied naturally or artificially, were responsible for the image on the Shroud, they would have changed color or burned at different rates during the fire, depending on their distance from the flames. A difference should be noticeable. However, no variation in the intensity of the image can be observed. In fact, Rogers said, the parts of the image that were in contact with the burned areas have apparently *"identical* color tone and density as parts of the image at the maximum distance from a discolored area."[4] This observation seemed to make it highly unlikely that an organic pigment was responsible for the image. (See photo 24).

Rogers also thought that these observations ruled out the possibility that the image had been formed by direct contact with a body. Such an image would have been formed by organic molecules and organic molecules would have changed color and burned at different rates depending on their distance from the flames during the fire. The Italian scientists also observed no "capillary flow"—the absorption of the image substance into the fibers of the threads on the microscopic level. This seemed to eliminate any inorganic compound, such as an ink.

The 1973 Italian commission produced no evidence that the "bloodstained" areas of the Shroud image actually contained blood. A standard hemoglobin test failed to find blood on the cloth. Other tests to detect blood also turned up negative. Some skeptics took this as evidence of forgery, but the Italian scientists who conducted the tests and other scientists who later examined their work regarded the tests as inconclusive. Blood proteins might have decayed over 2,000 years; the 1532 fire would have badly degraded them; and other events in the

Shroud's long history might have caused any blood on it to lose the characteristics by which it could be easily identified. Professor Georgio Frache, an Italian scientist who studied threads from the bloodstained areas, said that the tests would have been conclusive only if they showed the presence of blood. The fact that they did not detect blood, he concluded, still left the question open.[5]

Two other studies conducted in connection with the 1973 tests concerned the age of the Shroud; both strongly suggested that the Shroud is an ancient cloth, perhaps 2,000 years old.

Professor Gilbert Raes of Ghent Institute of Textile Technology studied threads that had been removed from the Shroud and confirmed an earlier conclusion made from photography that the weave and fabric of the linen are of a type known to have existed in Jesus' time. But Professor Raes found something else—traces of cotton among the linen fibers. He suggested that the Shroud had been woven on a loom also used for cotton.[6] This discovery helped pinpoint the location of the Shroud's manufacture: Cotton is not grown in Europe, but it grows abundantly in the Middle East.

The other study was conducted by Max Frei, a Swiss botanist and criminologist. Frei's microscopic investigation of the pollen grains on the Shroud identified pollen from plants which grow only in Palestine and Turkey.[7] This indicated that the cloth had been in these areas sometime during its existence. Frei's work is discussed in more detail in Chapter Two.

Perhaps the most significant result of the 1973 Italian studies was to get top-level scientists interested in the Shroud. Much serious scientific work was left to be done. In its final report, the Italian commission avoided making definitive conclusions and it skirted some of the most interesting issues. For example, the commission did not pursue its discovery that the image on the cloth is superficial in nature. In fact, the commission did not even inspect the reverse side of the cloth to see if the image was as superficial as it appeared to be in the thread samples. Although the Italian scientists made inconclusive tests for blood, they made no serious effort to identify those brown stains that looked so much like blood. Some of these limitations were caused by the way the commission was set up. The members of the commission, while competent in their fields, had never studied the Shroud before and they had never worked together. Perhaps their most obvious discovery was that the Shroud is far more complex than previously believed. It looked like the Shroud would yield the key to its secrets only grudgingly.

The Shroud of Turin Research Project

The next set of important discoveries about the Shroud was made by a group of scientists who in 1977 organized themselves as the Shroud of Turin Research Project. Working with the Enrie photographs and the observations made by the 1973 Italian commission, scientists working on the project made discoveries which both deepened the mystery of the Shroud and laid the theoretical groundwork for the definitive testing to come later.

The most intriguing of these findings was the discovery that the Shroud image contains three-dimensional data. This discovery, in some ways the most astounding and inexplicable of the Shroud's many mysteries, was made by John Jackson and Eric Jumper, two Air Force officers and physicists who studied the Shroud in their off hours from duties at the Air Force Weapons Laboratory in Albuquerque, New Mexico. Working with Bill Mottern, a colleague at the lab, Jackson and Jumper found that the brightness of the Shroud image is mathematically related to the distance of the body from the cloth. The image is brightest in areas where the body touched the cloth—for example, the nose, forehead, and eyebrows. The image is less intense in areas where the body did not touch the cloth—for example, the sides of the cheeks and the recessed areas of the eye sockets. This discovery indicated that the Shroud image was formed by a three-dimensional object. It also meant that the Shroud could not have been formed by direct contact, as by placing the cloth over a corpse or statue which had been heated or treated with pigment. The mystery was that parts of the body not in contact with the cloth also appear on the image, and the brightness of these non-contact areas *varies according to their distance from the cloth.*[8]

Because this ratio between body and cloth can be precisely described mathematically, Jackson and Jumper were able to reproduce a three-dimensional replica of the man buried in the Shroud. Scientists can do something similar with photographs of stars and planets, where the object is far enough away from the astronomer's lens that its distance measurably affects the intensity of the light image received. But a three-dimensional image cannot be created from any normal photograph, negative or positive. Modern lenses, films, and photographic papers are simply not sensitive enough to reproduce in a two-dimensional image the minute variations in light intensity emitted from different points on a three-dimensional object. Indeed, photographs analyzed the same way as the Shroud image fail to yield three-dimensional information. Eyes protrude, noses sink, and other distortions graphically testify to the uniqueness of the Shroud image.

Jackson and Jumper produced a three-dimensional replica of the man in the Shroud using a VP-8 Image Analyzer, a scientific instrument developed for planetary and stellar photographs. (See photos 15 and 16.) The very fact that they were able to generate a three-dimensional image from a two-dimensional photograph was in itself an intriguing piece of research, as well as a technological tour de force. However, the three-dimensional image opened up more of scientific scrutiny. Inspection of the three-dimensional picture suggested that the hair on the left side of the face seemed to drape over the edge of some invisible object, and something seemed to divide his beard. Jackson and Jumper proposed that this object was a chin band, a piece of linen cloth pulled up under the chin and tightened at the top of the head. Its purpose was to keep the mouth of the corpse closed; ordinarily, the jaw would open as rigor mortis set in. If this object was a chin band, it would be consistent with Jewish burial customs and with the gospel narrative of Jesus' burial. (See Chapter Four.)

The three-dimensional picture of the head of the man in the Shroud also revealed another surprise: small button-like objects had apparently been placed over his eyes. Jackson and Jumper thought they were coins, and suggested that they might be leptons of Pontius Pilate. Coins have been found in a skull from a Jewish cemetery dating from the first century A.D.[9] It is quite possible that it was the custom in Jesus' time to place coins over the eyes of the corpse in order to keep them closed. Francis L. Filas, professor at Loyola University of Chicago, thought he could identify the coin. After detailed studies, he concluded that the coin over the right eye of the man in the Shroud was a lepton minted in the time of Pontius Pilate.[10] While other investigators are awaiting more results, the existence of objects over the eyes of the man in the Shroud is another piece of evidence that the man in the Shroud was buried the way Jews were buried 2,000 years ago. (See Chapter Two and photos 6 and 7.)

Another investigation by members of the Shroud of Turin Research Project further reduced the probability that the image had been painted. Jean J. Lorre and Donald J. Lynn, scientists at the Jet Propulsion Laboratory in Pasadena, analyzed the Shroud image with some of the same computer-assisted techniques they had used to study images transmitted from the surface of Mars by the Viking lander in 1976. Lorre and Lynn could find no "directionality" to the image—that is, it had been applied to the surface of the cloth in a random and directionless fashion.[11] (See photo 23.) Any hand application of paint, dye, or any other foreign substance by a forger would have shown a characteristic pattern, no matter how carefully the artist painted or tried to cover his work.

To the curious scientists the implications of these findings from the Shroud of Turin Research Project began to look staggering. The Shroud image was not only a negative, but it was also superficial and it contained three-dimensional information. It appeared highly unlikely that anybody painted it. Finally, it seemed that the process that formed the image could not have been organic or natural in origin—it seems to have operated on inorganic coins as well as on dead flesh. The scientists could not imagine how such an image could be produced, either in the fourteenth century or in the twentieth.

In September, 1977, eight members of·the Shroud of Turin

Research Project went to Turin and proposed detailed testing to be performed on the cloth. The testing involved an extensive series of non-destructive tests in the various electromagnetic spectrum ranging from near infrared to X-rays. Walter McCrone and Associates of Chicago also submitted a separate proposal for carbon-14 dating. The proposals were designed to answer three major questions about the Shroud: (1) what is the image composed of? (2) how was the image formed? and (3) is there blood on the Shroud? The Americans brought copies of the proceedings of a research conference they conducted earlier in 1977 in Albuquerque, New Mexico. They also brought with them a three-dimensional replica of the Shroud image. (See photo 22.) The replica, along with the solid scientific work contained in the proceedings, apparently convinced the Italian authorities that the American proposals had great potential.

To prepare for new testing, the team carefully analyzed what was already known about the Shroud. Like all scientists working on a difficult problem, they relied on the work of previous researchers. The data they used included the photographs of Secondo Pia and Guiseppe Enrie, the observations of the 1969 secret commission (its report finally became available in 1976), the tests and conclusions drawn by the members of 1973 Italian panel, and their own work on the Shroud.

The analysts concentrated on the problem of the process that created the Shroud image. This would be the major focus of further testing. They enumerated the known characteristics of the Shroud image and asked whether the several theories for the image formation could account for them. The major characteristics of the Shroud image can be summarized as follows:

Superficiality. The image is essentially the discoloration of the very topmost fibers of the linen threads of the Shroud fabric. It did not appear to penetrate to the other side of the cloth, although the reverse side of the cloth had not been inspected for hundreds of years.

Detailed. The Shroud image is extraordinarily detailed. For example, scientists could count the number of scourge marks on the man's back, and even distinguish tiny scratches within the marks.

Thermally stable. The Shroud image was not affected by heat. That portion of the image that had been closest to the burns in the fire of 1532 seems identical with the color of the image far away from the blaze.

No pigment. It did not appear that any pigment formed the image. The image was created some other way.

Three-dimensional. This characteristic was perhaps the most surprising and mysterious of all. The intensity of the image varies according to the distance of the body from the cloth. The mathematical ratio was so precise that scientists could construct a three-dimensional replica of the man of the Shroud.

Negative. The image on the Shroud is a negative, that is, it is more detailed and lifelike when "printed" on photographic film.

Directionless. The process that formed the image operated in a non-directional fashion. It was not generated according to any directional pattern as it would have been if applied by hand.

Chemically stable. The yellow coloration composing the Shroud image cannot be dissolved, bleached, or changed by standard chemical agents.

Water stable. The Shroud was doused with water to extinguish the fire in 1532, but the image does not seem to have been affected.

These known characteristics of the Shroud image were then compared with the various theories for the formation process. To make such a comparison easier, we can align the characteristics and the theories in matrix form (see p. 68).

It should be emphasized that the scientists who made these judgments had not tested the Shroud themselves. Their deductions were based on photographs and on the recorded observations of other scientists, most notably those of the 1973 Italian commission. All these deductions still had to be tested. They were hypotheses, developed in large part to prepare for the intensive 1978 studies of the Shroud.

It is obvious from the chart that *painting* or application of some foreign substance appeared to be the least likely explanation for the Shroud image. An artist could have painted a

Comparison of Image Formation Theories with Image Characteristics

Theories Characteristics	Paint, Dye, or Powder	Direct Contact	Vapor	Direct Contact and Vapor	Heat or Light
Superficial	No	No	No	No	Yes
Detailed	No	No	No	Possible	Possible
Thermally Stable	No	Possible	No	Possible	Yes
No Pigment	No	Possible	Yes	Yes	Yes
3/D	No	No	No	No	Yes
Negative	Yes	Possible	Possible	Possible	Yes
Directionless	Possible	Possible	Yes	Yes	Yes
Chemically Stable	Possible	Possible	No	No	Yes
Water Stable	Possible	Possible	No	No	Yes

negative image, and it is possible that he used materials that would be stable over time and stable in water. Although it is highly unlikely, perhaps he could have applied pigment or dye with such fine brush strokes that computer analysis could not detect the pattern of his hand movements. On all other counts, however, the forgery theory falls short. Pigment would have penetrated past the superficial layers of the fibers. An artist could not have painted the image in such detail, paint would have been noticeably affected by the 1532 fire, and an artist could not have encoded three-dimensional information in his picture. Most paints would not be stable in heat and chemical solvents.

Another theory which did not seem to fit scientific observations is that of *direct contact* with the body. It had been suggested that the Shroud image was caused by a chemical reaction between the cloth and a real corpse in a real tomb, or by a clever forger who threw a cloth over a corpse, a treated statue, or a hot statue. An image produced by direct contact could have been directionless, stable in water, formed without pigment (if it was not forged), and possibly negative in nature. But a contact image would have been grossly distorted. You can verify this by smearing your face with charcoal and then pressing a cloth against it. The resulting image will not be a recognizable representation of your face. It certainly will not contain any three-dimensional information or the kind of detail the Shroud image contains. Neither would a direct contact image be a superficial image, and it also seemed to be eliminated on the same chemical and thermal grounds as a pigment or dye forgery; the organic molecules which would compose such an image would have been noticeably affected by the fire in 1532. Furthermore, every attempt to experimentally create an acceptable image by the use of direct contact between a body or statue has failed. It seemed to be impossible to create an acceptable impression of a three-dimensional object on a two-dimensional surface.

Paul Vignon's *vaporgraph theory* suffers from most of the same weaknesses as forgery and direct contact. Vignon, one will recall, suggested that the body projected an image of itself onto the Shroud by a chemical reaction between ammonia in the body sweat and a mixture of aloes and olive oil on the burial shroud. But an image formed this way would have reacted in some noticeable way to the fire and water of the 1532 fire. Neither would a vaporgraph image be superficial, detailed, or three-dimensional.

A *combination of effects* such as direct contact and vapors would not account for the image either. Eric Jumper conducted experiments to test this hypothesis, and found the results unacceptable.[12] He said that the direct-contact/vapor process did not produce any clear image at all. Jumper also found that the stain produced in his experiments penetrated the entire thread of the linen samples, and was therefore not superficial. There is also the matter of the objects which appear to lie on the eyes of the man in the Shroud. If the image was caused by vapors, how were the images of coins formed? Finally, such a combination would still not yield a three-dimensional image either.

All these theories of image formation abound with problems such as these, problems which revolve around the very nature of the image.

A few other theories for the formation of the image have been suggested but quickly discarded. One of these suggestions is that the image was formed by the so-called Kirlian effect, a much-disputed claim that living bodies contain mysterious "auras" which can be photographed under certain circumstances. Many scientists do not believe that the Kirlian effect even exists, and there is no plausible explanation of how it could account for the Shroud image. Others have looked with interest at an effect of thermonuclear explosions: the blast at Hiroshima apparently imprinted outlines of shadows on solid surfaces. But these are shadows, not images with resolution and detail. A thermonuclear blast would have destroyed the Shroud, and much of the surrounding area as well.

Enter the *scorch theory*. This hypothesis was first advanced in 1966 by Geoffrey Ashe, a British author who produced an image resembling that of the Shroud by exposing a piece of linen to radiant heat.[13] To the naked eye, the experimental scorch of a piece of linen seemed to resemble the color of the image on the Shroud. The Shroud image is sepia-colored; sepia is the color of linen when it undergoes the first stages of burning.

John Jackson, the Air Force physicist, realized that a ready-made test of the scorch hypothesis lay close at hand. The Shroud had been burned and scorched in the fire in 1532. If the color of the image areas of the Shroud resembled the color of the scorched areas, that would be an indication that the image might be a scorch. This, in fact, is what Jackson found when he analyzed a color photograph of the Shroud with a microdensitometer, an instrument that measures the densities of an image on a photographic film or plate. The instrument could detect no differences between the color of the Shroud image and the color of scorched areas. This suggested that the image on the Shroud could well be some kind of a scorch. Jackson pointed out that he used a photograph, not the Shroud itself, and that the photograph had not been taken for scientific purposes. Thus his findings had to be tentative until more exact scientific studies could be conducted.[14]

Nevertheless, the scorch hypothesis became the most likely theory of how the image on the Shroud was formed. At the scientific conference in 1977, Ray Rogers summed up the arguments for a scorch. He noted Jackson's finding that the color of the image area resembled the color of the heat damaged area. He pointed out that the image seemed to exist only on one side of the cloth. He cited another factor: the image density seemed to be related to the distance between the body and the cloth—the famous three-dimensional quality of the image. All this, Rogers said, suggests "rapid heating as the cause of the image." He said that if future testing did not identify any pigment on the cloth, and if no one found an organic stain that could have stained the cloth naturally, then the scorch theory was the only hypothesis left.

Eric Jumper, another Air Force physicist, thought that if the Shroud had been scorched, it would have to have been a very short burst of high energy radiation. He and John Jackson ran some experiments in which they scorched pieces of linen with lasers. Within a short time, an image appeared on the reverse side of the cloth almost as dark as the one on the front. Jumper thought that this ruled out any plausible forgery using a scorch. A forger could have heated a bronze statue or a flat plate and thrown a piece of linen over it, but the image this process produced would also be present on the back of the cloth. By contrast, their experiments showed that the radiation process would have to be very quick and very intense in order to scorch only the topmost layer of the linen fibers.[15]

John Jackson pointed out another problem with various theories of image formation. Employing sophisticated mathematical analysis, he showed that no reasonable physical mechanism could produce an image which was both three-dimensional *and* highly detailed. To achieve clarity, three-dimensionality had to be sacrificed. To produce an image that contained three-dimensional data, the image would not have been as detailed as the Shroud image is. Jackson thought his findings made it unlikely that the Shroud image was formed by some natural process involving diffusion of chemicals. He also said that a simple scorch caused by exposing the cloth to thermal radiation could not have produced a clear three-dimensional image either. However, Jackson said a scorch was still a possible explanation for the image because it could have been caused in some way other than by thermal radiation.[16]

These pre-1978 scientific studies of the Shroud seemed to be identifying a mystery. The scorch theory seemed to be the most plausible hypothesis for the formation of the image. But, if the image is a scorch, then it is unique. Scientists could not explain how the Shroud could have been scorched this way. Hence, while the scorch theory seemed to be the best, it was not totally without problems. The most significant of these problems was the absence of a natural formation process. However, since there are still many energy forms that are not yet fully understood, the issue was not closed. Nevertheless, a scorch would account for the vast majority of the known characteristics of the Shroud image much better than any other theory.

Where did this leave the pre-1978 question of the Shroud? Perhaps the most significant result of these early studies was the fact that a group of about forty esteemed scientists from various institutions became fascinated with a burial cloth that had long been thought to be a fraud. These scientists began detailed studies of the cloth on their own time and with their own money. Finally, they committed themselves to plan, develop, equip, and fund a series of tests in Turin without a single guarantee that such testing would indeed materialize. Furthermore, as each new fact became known, they expanded the scope of the effort to ensure that all facets of the question would be properly dealt with. All along the way these same individuals began to capture the interest and even the support of their peers and institutions.

The two years of preparation for the 1978 testing had clearly demonstrated that faith did not have to fear open, objective scientific inquiry. None of the scientists made extraordinary claims about the significance of their discoveries. Despite some fairly exciting findings, all publicly kept any religious beliefs and scientific facts separate. The Shroud of Turin Research Project made no sensationalistic press releases. Science limited its attention to scientific issues and to a clearly delineated listing of facts and theories. Interpretations of those facts were left for future, more definitive studies, and for individual evaluation.

The Shroud research before 1978 was useful to both religion and science. Science and religion did not marry. Neither did they declare war.

SIX

Science and the Shroud: Post-1978

BY ANY MEASURE, THE arrival of the members of the Shroud of Turin Research Project in Turin, Italy, in October, 1978, was an extraordinary occasion. Never before had a religious relic been examined so thoroughly by scientists. Never before had the church allowed an object of faith to be inspected with the neutral analytic tools of modern science. The incongruity of the occasion was obvious to most of the scientists as they unloaded their ultra-sophisticated testing equipment, worth millions of dollars, in the magnificent Renaissance reception room of the royal palace of the House of Savoy. Peter Rinaldi, the Italian-born priest who had done so much to win approval for the testing, commented that it was fitting for the princes of American science to do their work in such princely surroundings.

Most members of the project team had more practical matters on their minds. Everyone wanted to complete the long-awaited tests as quickly as possible. Months of difficult negotiations over the team's test plans had preceeded its arrival in Turin. The church regarded the whole matter of scientific testing of the Shroud as so sensitive that it would not even allow the team to confirm or deny that the testing would take place. The team's arrival had also been preceeded by difficulties with customs officials, some lost camera equipment, and harrassment from the news media. Anastasio Ballestrero, the archbishop of Turin, had approved the testing with the request that he be the first to know if the scientists determined that the image on the Shroud was a forgery. Some members of the team felt that a delegation would have to break the bad news to Archbishop Ballestrero soon, and they worried about the impact this might have on the millions of faithful around the world who revere the Shroud of Turin. Most of the scientists thought that the tests would reveal that the Shroud was not authentic.

However, the project team did not find that the Shroud image was a fake. Consistent with the history of scientific examination of the Shroud, the 1978 results in a sense only deepened the mystery of the cloth. The project team made few conclusions during the five days of testing in October, 1978. It has taken nearly three years for dozens of scientists from the United States and Europe to examine this data in their laboratories and to draw some conclusions from it. This chapter discusses the results of these tests and presents the conclusions.

General Properties of the Shroud Image

Microscopic examination of the Shroud in 1978 yielded the first complete technical description of the Shroud image. What the human eye sees as the image is a yellow discoloration of the linen fibers which make up the threads of the cloth. Approximately one or two hundred of these fibers are woven together to compose each thread. The threads are an average of .15 mm in diameter. The image is quite superficial, that is, only the very topmost fibers in each thread are discolored in the image areas of the cloth. The image does not penetrate through the individual thread. In most places, the yellow discoloration extends only two or three fibers deep into the thread structure. (See photo 19.) The microscopic examination also revealed that the image is monochromatic: the yellow discoloration of the fibers is the same color throughout the image. What the eye sees as differences in color are actually differences in the density of the discolored fibers. In other words, the "darker" areas of the image are not yellower. They appear darker because they contain more discolored fibers than the lighter areas.

These density differences are related to the distance between the cloth and the body underneath it. This is the famous three-dimensional property of the image. For example, the forehead of the image is darker than the eye sockets beneath it. The three-dimensionality was fully confirmed by the photographs taken in 1978. There had been suspicions that this three-dimensional property was a peculiarity of the black-and-white photographs of the image taken by Giuseppe Enrie in 1931.[1] Vernon Miller, the project team photographer with the Brooks Institute of Photography in Santa Barbara, California, took high-resolution photographs under controlled conditions in 1978. Analysis of these photographs in the VP-8 Image Analyzer showed the same density variations related to cloth-body distance that John Jackson and Eric Jumper had discovered several years earlier using the 1931 photographs.

The scientists also took note of the faintness of the image. The image on the Shroud is much easier to see at a distance than it is at close range. Peering at the Shroud from a distance of a few inches, the scientists were hardly able to see the difference between the image and non-image areas. Fifteen to twenty feet away, however, they were able to discern almost all of the details. This curious phenomenon is a product of the human eye. The Shroud image lacks sharp boundaries between image and non-image areas, while the eye is designed to enhance edge contrasts. The technical term for this property of the eye is "lateral neural inhibition."[2] The eye can see edges of a faint image when the image is compressed into a small portion of the total field of vision—as when one stands far away from the Shroud. However, the same image appears faint and indistinct when viewed at close range.

These observations about the general properties of the image have several obvious implications for the study of the process that formed it. The process had to be one that changed only the topmost fibers of the threads. It also had to be one which varied the density of the yellow fibers rather than the intensity of the color. It had to be able to create an image even where the cloth did not touch the body. Finally, the fact that the image can barely be seen up close meant that it would be very difficult for an artist who was trying to paint the image to check the progress of his work.

The scientists of the Shroud of Turin Research Project arrived in Turin primarily seeking answers to three questions: (1) What is the image composed of? (2) What was the process that formed it? (3) What is the composition of the "bloodstains"? The microscopic examination of the image answered much about the first question. The image, very simply, is a yellow discoloration of the tiny linen fibers which compose the threads of the Shroud. A smaller and separate problem was the composition of the "bloodstains" on the Shroud. We will look at the team's findings in this area before turning to the question of the process that formed the image.

The Bloodstains

The "blood" areas on the Shroud have attracted considerable attention since the first color photographs of the cloth became available. It appeared that blood had flowed from the man's feet, wrists, and side. (See photos 10, 11, 25, and 26.) The reddish-brown stains appear to be quite anatomically correct, as one would expect if a man had bled after being stabbed in the side and nailed through his wrists and feet. The edges of these stains are also precisely defined. If the Shroud actually covered a real corpse, one wonders how the cloth was removed without smearing and dislodging the edges of the clotted blood.

When they arrived in Turin in 1978, the scientists did not know whether the "bloodstains" were really blood. Members of the 1973 Italian commission had removed small pieces of thread from the stained areas and tested them for the presence of hemoglobin, the iron-containing protein that gives blood its red color. These tests turned up negative, but the Italians considered these results inconclusive.[3] Much could have happened to degrade the structure of blood over 2,000 years; if the stains were blood, hemoglobin might be present in quantities too small for the tests to detect. Also, the 1532 fire could certainly have affected the hemoglobin, which can be altered by heat.

The 1978 team hoped to settle the blood question once and for all by examining the bloodstained areas with a full battery of optical tests throughout the electromagnetic spectrum. (See Chart 2, Appendix D.) The most important and conclusive work was done by John Heller and Alan Adler in their laboratory at the New England Institute.[4] Heller and Adler examined several "sticky tape" samples which contained pieces of "bloodstained" fibrils. They looked at the spectrum of the visible light transmitted from these samples under a microscope, a test known as microspectrophotometry. The results suggested that hemoglobin was a component of the color. To further test this possibility, Heller and Adler removed the iron from the samples and tried to isolate porphyrin, a component of blood which fluoresces red under an ultraviolet light. Indeed, the substance which the chemists isolated from the samples fluoresced red under ultraviolet light. This confirmed that the substance was porphyrin, and thus strongly indicated that the bloodstained areas really were blood.

A further indication that blood was present on the Shroud came from the ultraviolet fluorescence photographs taken by Vernon Miller and Samuel Pellicori. Blood itself does not fluoresce. However, when Miller and Pellicori studied their ultraviolet fluorescence photographs of the blood areas, they discovered a light fluorescent margin around the edges of several of the bloodstained areas. These areas were the side wound, the nail wound in the wrist, and the blood flow at the right foot on the dorsal image.

The probable explanation for this unexpected discovery is that the fluorescent margins were blood serum, the colorless fluid part of the blood. Miller and Pellicori showed in the laboratory that blood serum on linen does fluoresce moderately. Thus, it is likely that the fluorescent margins are blood serum which had become separated from whole blood before or after the man's death.

Several other tests confirmed the presence of blood on the Shroud. Protein, a component of blood, was detected in the blood areas, although no protein was found elsewhere on the cloth. X-ray fluorescence examination found that iron, a component of blood, was present in the blood area. The team's summary of research concluded that the bloodstained areas were very probably stained by real blood.[5]

Image Formation

The most interesting and complex question by far was the problem of image formation. How did the image get on the cloth? What could have created an image with such unusual properties?

The scientists arranged the various theories of image formation into two groups: first, that the image was artificially made; and, second, that a natural process had caused it. Several difficulties cropped up with this conceptual scheme. Since no one knew exactly how the image came to be on the cloth, the initial division between artificial-image and natural-image theories seemed arbitrary, or at least premature. One of the theories considered most seriously by the team—the suggestion that a sensitizing material had produced the image—had to be considered under both categories because it could have been both a natural process and a forger's tool. The most controversial result of this theoretical arrangement was the team's classification of scorch theories under the artificial-image grouping. If the image proved to be a scorch, they reasoned, it *had* to be artificial. If it was a natural scorch, the scientists would have to explain how a dead body could have given off enough heat or light to scorch a linen cloth. This they could not do.

Thus the division of image formation theories into these two categories implied that the project team ruled out at the start the possibility that the image had a supernatural origin, or at least an origin that could not be understood by science in its current state of development. Perhaps scientists could not have proceeded any other way, but this assumption may have contributed to the tentativeness of the team's final conclusions. In the end, it did not appear that the Shroud image was either artificial or natural. But before they reached any conclusions, the scientists diligently examined all the possibilities.

Theory: The Image Is a Painting. It had been thought for centuries, at least by some, that the image of a dead man on the Shroud of Turin had been painted by some clever artist in the fourteenth century. This was the accusation made by Pierre D'Arcis in 1389 and repeated by Catholic intellectuals in the nineteenth and early twentieth centuries. The painting hypothesis became less and less tenable as scientists learned more about the properties of the image, and the project team hoped to finally determine whether the painting hypothesis had any validity. This they managed to do, and the team reached one of its most definite conclusions on this point. It concluded that the image unquestionably does not reside in any kind of foreign material applied to the cloth.

The battery of microscopic and optical tests (see chart 2, Appendix D) decisively disposed of the painting theory. The most important of these tests for the painting theory was direct microscopic observation. Other tests included X-ray fluorescence, which measured the composition of the elements in the Shroud; and X-radiography, which observed changes in the density of the Shroud. Other tests which could find foreign substances on the Shroud were photoelectric spectrophotometry, photoelectric and photographic fluorescence, and direct observation of the Shroud in visible light.

The direct microscopic examination of the Shroud revealed no evidence of a painting. No pigment particles were found on the Shroud under 50X magnification. The yellowish color of the fibers did not saturate the cloth in any image area—even the darkest. Nowhere were the cloth fibers cemented together, as a pigment would have done. There was no evidence for capillary flow—that is, the flowing of liquids throughout the cloth on a microscopic level.

The scientists also examined thirty-two "sticky tape" samples taken from all over the Shroud. These tapes were pressed

onto the cloth in image and non-image areas and then removed, with loose particles adhering to them. Under the
microscope, it was revealed that the Shroud had collected a
number of miscellaneous materials over the years. These included insect parts, pollen, wax, wool, red silk, modern syn-
thetic fibers, and several types of red and black particles. Most
importantly, the tapes also removed fragments of fiber, some
yellowed from the image areas, and some from non-image
areas.

These tapes, including the fiber particles adhering to many
of them, were subjected to more intense microscopic analysis
than was possible with the Shroud itself. The scientists were
able to observe the structure of the linen fibers in great detail.
The fibers consisted of plant cells joined end-to-end. They look
somewhat like bamboo under the microscope. The joints were
very clear and well-defined, and showed no sign of having
been coated by paint or any other foreign material.

John Heller and Alan Adler, the chemists at the New England Institute, conducted a series of tests on the image fibers
from the sticky tape samples in order to learn more about the
chemical nature of the yellow discoloration.[6] They applied five
different tests for the presence of protein; all came up negative,
with the exception of tape samples from the "blood" areas.
Other tests to detect inorganic compounds turned up some
iron and calcium on the Shroud, but not enough to account for
the yellowing of the linen fibers. Several tests to detect the
presence of organic dyes and stains on the fibers turned up
negative. Heller and Adler could not extract the yellow color
with acids, bases, or organic solvents. Neither could they bleach
it out with strong oxidants.

The chemists concluded that the image was not caused by an
applied pigment or any other foreign substance, but was the
result of the degradation of cellulose, the plant material in
linen fibers. The cellulose fibers in the image areas had been
dehydrated, in contrast to the wholly hydrated fibers in the
non-image areas. The dehydrated fibers in the image areas
reflected light faintly in the visible region of the spectrum. This
is what caused the visible image.

The examination of the sticky tape samples produced one interesting controversy. Walter McCrone, a microscopist who is not a member of the research team, obtained some sticky tape samples from a team member for examination. McCrone noted the presence of a small quantity of iron oxide, a red-colored substance, on some of the sticky tape samples. He speculated that an artist might have used iron oxide to enhance the image. Because there is only a very small quantity of iron oxide on the entire Shroud, McCrone postulated that the "red pigment" might have been applied in a very dilute solution. But McCrone went even further. Pigment is always applied in a medium such as wax or oil. McCrone's most controversial assertion was that the discoloration of the fibers may have been caused by the yellowing of the paint medium with age.[7]

Examination of the tape samples and other observations by team members found no evidence for McCrone's theory. In their exhaustive battery of chemical tests, Heller and Adler uncovered no signs of any medium that a medieval artist could have used. Under the microscope, there was no sign that any kind of liquid had been applied to the fibers.[8] McCrone's theory was finally disposed of by the X-ray fluorescence and visible light examination of the Shroud, and by microchemcial studies. These tests determined that there is not nearly enough iron oxide on the cloth to account for even an enhancement of the image.[9] McCrone's thesis, like other fraud hypotheses, is finally disproven by the three-dimensional, superficial, non-directional nature of the Shroud image, as well as by the absence of any plateaus or saturation points in the image. It might also be pointed out that submicron iron oxide has only been available for about 200 years, thereby further ruling out its use in medieval painting (see Appendix A1.)

The project team's summary of research concluded that the iron oxide evidence was "irrelevant to the image formation problem."[10] The team found McCrone wrong. The iron oxide does *not* account for the image.

John Jackson, a physicist, proposed a plausible explanation for the presence of small amounts of iron oxide on the Shroud. Jackson noted that the iron oxide was present in especially large concentrations in the blood areas. This was not surprising because iron is a major component of blood. Jackson thought that small amounts of iron oxide could have been distributed throughout the Shroud if the cloth had been simply folded and unfolded several times. This must have happened, because we know the Shroud was kept in a folded state at the time of the 1532 fire. (In more recent times, the Shroud has been rolled up in a cylindrical fashion and covered with a red silk casing.)

The other tests conducted on the Shroud in 1978 confirmed the finding that there was no foreign matter present on the Shroud in sufficient quantity to account for the image. The X-ray fluorescence test would have detected inorganic pigments containing iron, arsenic, lead, or other heavy metal compounds. It found none.[11] Low-energy radiography normally detects density variations in paintings when the pigment is present in large amounts. This examination found density differences in the cloth, but none which correspond to the image. The density differences were slight variations in the thickness of the cloth itself.[12] Two different instruments beamed light at the Shroud and measured how various parts of the cloth reflected the light. Dyes, stains, and pigments reflect light in characteristic ways, but no signs of them were found anywhere on the Shroud.[13] Two other tests measured the fluorescence properties of the cloth. Sometimes different materials can be identified by the way they fluoresce, but generally no material on the Shroud fluoresced differently than the cloth itself.[14] In fact, the image appeared to reduce the fluorescent properties of the underlying cloth, something that would happen if the upper layer of fiber was dehydrated.

Some other observations added to the high improbability of the painting hypothesis. Before the project team arrived in Turin, Ray Rogers had pointed out that if the Shroud image was a painting, the heat from the 1532 fire and the water used to extinguish it would have visibly affected the image. Since he could observe no heat or water effects in photographs, Rogers thought it unlikely that the image was a painting.[15] The team's inspection of the cloth in Turin found Rogers to be correct.

There were no differences in color density between the image areas closest to the burns and those farthest away from them. Neither did the water used to extinguish the fire affect the image in any way. The scientists could also see no brush marks or directionality to the image, two conclusions that had been tentatively reached on the basis of photographs. (See Appendix A1.)

Fraud hypotheses are finally disproven by the three-dimensional, superfical, and non-directional nature of the Shroud image, plus the lack of any image plateaus or saturation points. In particular, fraud cannot account for the three-dimensional property. An artificial formation process would not have created an image in areas where the cloth was untouched by any contact. Neither can fraud explain the superficial, non-saturated surface phenomenon of the Shroud image.

The Shroud of Turin Research Project found that Pierre D'Arcis was wrong: the image on the Shroud was not a painting. The summary of research said that, "we have found no evidence to suggest that the visible image results from a pigment on the cloth. In this regard, the data are quite internally consistent."[16]

Theory: The Shroud Was Changed by Chemicals. The team considered other theories of how the cellulose in the linen fibers could have been yellowed without the use of pigment. Several theories held that the chemical composition of the cellulose in the fibers had been changed by a chemical which was later washed off or otherwise removed. One problem with these theories was that the microscopic and electromagnetic examination of the Shroud revealed that no chemical was present on the cloth in any appreciable quantity. Thus these theories were somewhat speculative and involved and some creative laboratory work to test them.

One possibility, largely theoretical, was that someone had painted the Shroud image with acid. Concentrated sulphuric acid does yellow cellulose, but only if it is quickly neutralized in order to avoid grave damage to the cloth. It seems virtually impossible to paint this way. The scientists who experimented with this technique also found it very difficult to reproduce the image's superficiality and the lack of image saturation. They could not control the penetration of the acid into the cloth. Also, acid painting produces densities which differ from the densities of the yellow stains observed on the Shroud. Neither could acid painting reproduce the three-dimensionality of the image. The scientists called these attempts to create an image with acid "rather disappointing."[17]

Samuel Pellicori, a scientist at the Santa Barbara Research Center, proposed a more complex theory involving chemicals.[18] Pellicori experimented with the idea that a catalyst had sensitized the Shroud to produce a "latent" image. This image was later "developed" by heat or by the aging of the linen, thus producing the visible image.

In his laboratory, Pellicori baked samples of linen in an oven at 150° Centrigrade for seven-and-a-half hours, a technique which simulated aging. The linen yellowed somewhat and it had reflectance and fluorescence characteristics that resembled those of the non-image areas of the Shroud. Pellicori then applied thin coatings of skin secretions, myrrh, and olive oil to different areas of his samples and put them back in the oven for three-and-a-half hours. These treated areas grew yellower than the discolored background of the cloth. Could a man's body have "sensitized" the Shroud with skin secretions, and could this image have been gradually "developed" by hundreds of years of aging? Could an artist have employed this technique?

Pellicori's experiment did account for some of the observed characteristics of the Shroud image. Of all the hypotheses for a chemically-induced image formation, only Pellicori's idea actually showed how some applied substance could yellow cellulose fibers in way resembling the Shroud image. His theory thus attracted much attention and some ingenious development. However, Pellicori's experiment looked better in the laboratory than it did either as a forger's technique or as a way that a real corpse could have imprinted an image of itself on a linen cloth. For one thing, the examination of the Shroud showed no trace of the sensitizing materials which would have caused the image areas of the cloth to darken. Since the latent image theory requires such chemical additions, their absence on the Shroud is an important shortcoming. Another problem was one that cropped up even in the laboratory. It proved to be very difficult to apply the sensitizing agents thinly enough so that they resided only on the topmost fibers of the cloth threads.[19] It is highly improbable that an artist could have applied the substance so thinly, or that a real corpse could have sensitized only the topmost layers of a Shroud which lay over and under it. Superficiality is thus another problem for the latent image theory.

But a more serious problem arose when the scientists began to think in detail about how the sensitizing agents proposed by Pellicori were actually applied to the cloth. The difficulty, once again, was the way the yellow fibers varied in density according to the distance between the cloth and the parts of the body—the three dimensional property. Pellicori's sensitizing agents could only have been applied to the cloth by direct contact. If so, how could the discoloration which these agents caused show any kind of cloth-body distance relationship in areas where the cloth did not touch the body? Even Pellicori admits that three-dimensionality is a major objection to his hypothesis.

John German, a scientist at the Air Force Weapons Laboratory and a member of the team, proposed an ingenious variant to the latent image model.[20] German suggested that the Shroud was originally very stiff when applied to the corpse, but gradually drooped in the damp atmosphere of the tomb. Eventually, all parts of the cloth where an image is observed touched the appropriate parts of the body. Since the raised parts of the body would have been in contact with the cloth longer than the lower parts, the oil or other sensitizing agent on the high points of the body would have been in contact with the cloth longer than the sensitizing agent on the other parts. German suggested that the high points yellowed the cloth more densely and the low points less so, according to the length of time the cloth had touched them.

However, German's idea was not able to account for the actual variations in image density observed on the Shroud. The face of the man in the Shroud provides one example of the theory's limitations. The whole face appears on the Shroud in great detail, yet the contour variations on a human face are very great. To account for the facial image under the German hypothesis, the cloth would have to have touched every part of the face. To do this, however, the cloth would have to be exceptionally flexible, much more flexible than the Shroud actually is. The German theory also required the sensitizing agent to be very sensitive to time. The Shroud displays very fine details and shadings. Could a sensitizing agent, applied to a stiff burial shroud as it drooped in a damp atmosphere, work with such precision? It seems unlikely. Neither did the Pellicori-German hypothesis seem able to account for the appearance of the hair on the Shroud image. And what about the objects over the eyes? If the sensitizing agent was perspiration or body oil, how did coins or shards of pottery appear on the image?

Indeed, it seemed highly unlikely that any kind of direct contact could account for the Shroud image. The fundamental problem can be demonstrated in a simple experiment mentioned earlier. Rub a layer of charcoal all over your face, press a white cloth against it, and pull it away. The resulting image will be grossly distorted. This illustrates an inherent limitation in attempting to reproduce a three-dimensional object on a two-dimensional surface by direct contact.

The Pellicori-German theory attempts to overcome this limitation by postulating direct contact over time. It suggests that very small differences in pressure will be able to reproduce details and shadings by delivering minutely differing quantities of sensitizing material to the cloth. In other words, the theory depends on pressure—the time of contact between the cloth and parts of the body.

However, pressure could not have been a significant factor in the Shroud image. The Shroud contains an image of the man's back as well as his front. The rear or dorsal image is slightly more distinct than the front (especially under ultraviolet flourescence), but the difference is not great. However, the pressure differences on the cloth were very great. The man buried in the cloth was lying on his back with his full weight pressing on the Shroud. Yet the only pressure on the cloth covering his front came from the weight of the cloth itself. The process that formed the image may have been affected by pressure but must have been essentially independent of pressure. Some mechanism other than contact caused the image on the Shroud.

The fact that the Pellicori-German hypothesis depends on pressure differences is a final reason why it could not explain the pressure-independent image on the Shroud. They proposed a way that the Shroud could have been yellowed, but there was no plausible way for the latent image to be created, either by a forger or by a real corpse. As John Jackson stated, a direct contact "could not have been responsible for generating the Shroud image."[21]

Theory: The Image Is a Vaporgraph. The scientific team then turned to an older idea of chemically-induced image formation. In fact, it was the oldest theory, the first to be proposed by a serious scientist after it became clear that the Shroud was not obviously a painting. This was Paul Vignon's vaporgraph theory.[22] Vignon, a French artist and biologist, suggested that the image was created by a chemical reaction between ammonia on the body and aloes and olive oil on the cloth. The crucified man buried in the Shroud would have perspired a morbid sweat containing urea, and the urea would have fermented into carbon dioxide and ammonia. Vignon suggested that the ammonia diffused from the corpse to the cloth, where it reacted with the aloes and olive oil to produce a stain. Vignon proposed this vaporgraph theory in the first decades of the twentieth century, and it gained wide acceptance among people who thought the Shroud might be genuine.

The scientists found grave problems with the vaporgraph theory. There seemed to be no way it could account for the high resolution in detail in the image. Vapors diffusing through space simply cannot be that precise. They do not travel upward in straight or parallel lines but rather diffuse in the air. Chemists also concluded that morbid sweat on a corpse would not have produced enough ammonia to cause the reaction which the vaporgraph theory required. Even if it did, such a chemical reaction would have permeated the threads of the cloth. As noted many times previously, the image is superficial and without any saturation. The yellowish color did not permeate or reach any plateaus. The cloth would also have to be damp for Vignon's chemical reaction to have occurred. This meant that it would have clung tightly to the body in many places, and the resulting image would have been grossly distorted.

Additionally, vaporgraph theories are refuted by properties of the Shroud image such as its three-dimensional nature, its shading and its stability in both heat and water. Also, the scientific investigation found that there is no foreign material from such chemical reactions as would be required, as well as no gaseous diffusion or capillary flow in the image, as a vaporgraph would produce.

Chemists considered a number of other chemical reactions involving natural products which could produce stains on linen. All of them had the same limitations of Vignon's model. Almost all of them would have been visibly affected by the heat and water from the 1532 fire. They would have permeated the cloth, and none could reproduce the high resolution and the three-dimensional properties of the image. Likewise, such alternatives do not produce a clear image and are further refuted by the absence of needed chemicals, diffusion, or capillary flow on the Shroud. As the summary of research states, "We view the evidence to be quite conclusive in ruling out the Vignon vaporgraphic theory as an image formation hypothesis."[23] Jumper and Rogers add that "Gas diffusion in the image formation process is not possible,"[24] thereby ruling out this and related hypotheses (see Appendix A2).

Theory: The Image Is a Scorch. The scientific team arrived in Turin in 1978 already suspecting that the image on the Shroud could well be some kind of scorch. The scorch theory had become the leading candidate for image formation partly because other theories seemed improbable and partly because the image looked like a scorch in photographs available before 1978. Cellulose yellows in the first stages of burning. If the heat and timing are carefully controlled, an experimental scorch can yellow cellulose fibers the way those on the Shroud are yellowed. Furthermore, a known scorch—the burns from the 1532 fire—lay right on the cloth, and the image resembled it. Analysis of color photographs prior to 1978 indicated that the image and the fire scorch have similar optical properties. A scorch has several other properties which the Shroud image also possesses. The image was not affected by the heat of the 1532 fire or by the water thrown on the Shroud to extinguish it. Neither heat nor water would affect a scorch in any way.[25]

The 1978 observations largely confirmed this pre-1978 theorizing. The ultraviolet and visible light reflectance tests showed that the image and the fire scorches reflected light in a similar way.[26] Chart 1 in Appendix D compares the reflectance properties of the image and fire scorches; the two curves agree within the margins of experimental error. The image and the scorch areas also reduced the background fluorescence of the cloth at a similar rate.[27]

However, the optical properties of the Shroud image and the fire scorches are not identical. The fire scorches are visually redder than the body image, and the two areas of the cloth fluoresce somewhat differently under ultraviolet light.[28] The team thought that these differences would be present if scorches had occurred under different conditions. In 1532, the Shroud was burned while sealed inside a metal box. Such a scorch, occurring in a substantially oxygen-free environment, would be visibly redder and would have different fluorescent properties than a scorch which occurred in the presence of oxygen. Indeed, Vernon Miller and Samuel Pellicori demonstrated this fact experimentally. They burned cellulose in an oxygen-depleted environment, and the scorch this experiment produced fluoresced in a way similar to those of the fire-damaged areas of the Shroud. It thus seemed probable to many members of the team that the image on the Shroud is a scorch, slightly different than the known scorches on the Shroud, but a scorch nonetheless.[29]

If the image was a scorch, how did it get on the cloth? This question proved to be very difficult to answer in scientific terms. The problem was finding what the Schwalbe and Rogers summary of research called a "technologically credible image transfer mechanism."[30] This was the main objection to the scorch hypothesis before 1978, and it remained the major objection after the testing and analysis were completed. Not all of the scientists agree with the scorch thesis, and many members of the scientific team stopped well short of imagining that a corpse emitted enough light and heat to scorch a burial shroud. Indeed, the team's summary of research classified the scorch hypothesis in the category of artificial-image theories. In other words, a chief issue for some was attempting to view the Shroud image in strictly natural terms. As we will see in Chapters Eleven and Twelve, this may not be fully possible.

Before 1978, Ray Rogers, a chemist at the Los Alamos National Laboratory, suggested that the Shroud could have been scorched by rapid heating.[31] On further study, the scientists decided that a short, intense burst of light or heat—the so-called "flash photolysis" hypothesis—was hard to support. They could not produce an acceptable scorch in the laboratory with flash lamps, and ultraviolet, visible, and infrared light lasers. Very short flashes of energy did scorch linen superficially, but the resulting scorches looked very different than the image on the Shroud. The short burst experiments were also very hard to control. They easily caused damage to the cloth of a kind not observed on the Shroud.

The scientists thought that a more likely scorch hypothesis would involve a light scorch at moderate temperatures. If the image was a scorch, the evidence suggested that it was done relatively slowly.

An issue with the scorch hypothesis remains to be solved. Before the 1978 testing, John Jackson had done theoretical work which produced a dilemma in considering how a three-dimensional object under the Shroud of Turin could have produced the image on the cloth by scorching.[32] Jackson showed mathematically that simple radiation emitted by a three-dimensional object could not have produced the density shading and resolution observed in the Shroud image. He thought that acceptable shading and resolution could have been produced if the radiation source varied in intensity or if something in the area between the cloth and the body caused variations in the heat or light. However, such a variation would have distorted the image. In other words, a process which would have produced acceptable shading and resolution would distort the image. A process which would have produced a clear image would not yield the correct shading and resolution. However, Jackson points out that this dilemma is not necessarily insoluable. He says that the "view that the image is the result of a scorch is not necessarily incompatible with this result because mechanisms other than isotropic thermal radiation could scorch cloth."[33]

Conclusions about Image Formation

The conclusions of the Shroud of Turin Research Project about the process which formed the image on the Shroud have a tentative aspect to them. The team's strongest conclusion was a negative one: that the image did not result from applied pigment. The testing showed no evidence for any foreign material which could account for the image. On the positive side, it achieved a chemical description of the image which ruled out pigment, dye, stains, powder, or ink. The image consists of yellowed cellulose fibers, which have been yellowed by some sort of dehydration process.

The scientists could not make up their collective mind about how this dehydration of the cellulose fibers occurred. The two hypotheses considered most seriously were scorching and a chemical reaction involving sensitizing material applied to the cloth by direct contact. Both theories were carefully tested. The scorch theory has relatively fewer problems than the sensitized or "latent image" hypothesis. The scorch theory had difficulty with the image resolution and shading, although Jackson reported that this difficulty might not arise in all scorch processes. The difficulties with the latent image hypothesis were more numerous. Besides resolution and shading, no sensitizing material was found on the Shroud. It was also difficult to imagine how the sensitizing material could have been applied in a way that accounts for the superficiality of the image, its lack of saturation points, its clarity, or its completeness. In addition, the application of the oil or perspiration necessary to sensitize the cloth depends on highly precise pressure variations, but the observed properties of the Shroud image seem clearly to be independent of pressure. Finally, the latent image theory cannot account for the three-dimensionality of the image.

So far a *completely natural explanation* of the image of the man buried in the Shroud has eluded the scientists. The great problem with all the theories is what the scientists call "an image transfer mechanism." In other words, they are reasonably confident they understand what the Shroud image is, but producing a completely physical explanation in another matter. As we will see in Chapters Eleven and Twelve, it may be that the Shroud image might not be explicable in purely natural terms.

Nevertheless, the scorch hypothsis is more probable than the latent image theory. The characteristics of the Shroud image are the characteristics of a scorch. The observations of Gilbert and Gilbert indicate this. In their laboratory, Heller and Adler verified the probability that the image fibrils reacted as if they were caused by heat.[34] A scorch of a linen cloth at moderate temperatures (less than 280° Centigrade) dehydrates the cloth and produces conjugation. It is significant that dehydration and conjugation, along with oxidation, are the primary characteristics of the cellulose fibers of the Shroud image. In addition, a scorch could account for the superficiality, unsaturation, thermal stability, and stability in water of the Shroud image. Thus both the scientific observations and study of the characteristics of the Shroud image suggest that the image was probably formed by a light scorch.

One must conclude that the scientists' work made a forgery virtually impossible. By ruling out a painting, the team stripped a hypothetical forger of the tools that would have been most available to him in the fourteenth century—pigments, dyes, powders, and inks. The latent image hypothesis would require him to work with nearly invisible oils or chemicals, in addition to all the other problems noted above. Neither was there any technically credible way that a forger could have scorched the cloth.

As a team, the Shroud of Turin Research Project avoided the question of the identity of the man in the Shroud. The question of the man's identity did not even arise in the team's report. Historical data was usually considered only when it involved technical questions such as the circumstances of the 1532 fire. Scriptural and archaeological evidence were generally not major concerns either. This is somewhat understandable in that physics, chemistry, and medicine are not actually equipped to address such issues.

For those of us who do want to address the question of the man's identity, it is important to stress the fact that the 1978 research provides considerable evidence that the image on the Shroud was formed by a real corpse in a real tomb. The scientists could not decide how this happened in a pure "technologically credible" way, but the fact that this happened is the inescapable conclusion of their work. The image could not have been done by a forger. The scorch hypothesis is more probable than the latent image hypothesis. At any rate, the man buried in the Shroud was a real man—a first-century Jew crucified by Romans in a fashion exactly paralleling the gospel accounts of how the Romans crucified Jesus Christ.

1

2

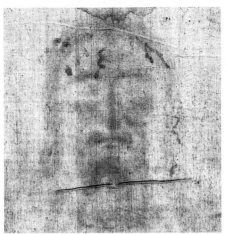

3

Where was the Shroud before the mid-fourteenth century? Clues come from Byzantine art. Before the sixth century, Christ's face was painted in many ways, but then artists began to render it in a way uncannily resembling the face of the man buried in the Shroud of Turin. The noticeable similarities between the Shroud face and the fresco Christ Pantocrator **(above)** from Daphni, Greece, are a "V" feature at the bridge of the nose, heavily accented eyes, a streak across the forehead, a hairless area between the lower lip and beard, and both hair and beard parted in the middle. These same features are visible in a copy of the Mandylion **(left)**, an image of Christ revered in Byzantium until it disappeared in the sack of Constantinople in 1204. Some historians think the Mandylion and the Shroud were the same. The cloth may have been brought to Europe by the Knights Templars, a religious order of European knights which was active in the Crusades. This theory gained support in 1951 when a Templar image of Christ was discovered in a cottage in Templecombe, England **(lower left)**. It too remarkably resembles both the Mandylion and the Shroud face.

Duke Louis of Savoy, a pious and ambitious prince, acquired the Shroud in 1453 from its owner, the widow of a minor French noble. The current owner is Louis' descendent Umberto II, the exiled King of Italy. The Savoy princes brought the Shroud to Turin in 1578 when they moved their capital there, and in 1694 they gave it a permanent home in the Royal Chapel of Turin **(above)**. For security reasons, the Shroud is exhibited infrequently—about once each generation.

Textile experts say the Shroud's herringbone twill weave pattern **(left)** is of costly manufacture. This style has been found in other first-century weaving, but it was not common. In 1976, a Belgian scholar discovered traces of cotton among the linen threads, suggesting that the Shroud was woven on a loom also used for cotton. Since cotton is not grown in Europe, the Shroud was probably made in the Middle East.

6

The Man of the Shroud appears to have been buried with coins over his eyes, a first-century Jewish custom. Francis L. Filas, professor at Loyola University in Chicago, believes he can date the Shroud by matching an ancient coin with the shape and detail of these objects. The coin is a lepton **(above)**, minted by Pontius Pilate in Palestine in 31 or 32 A.D. The photo below compares a lepton of a slightly different shape with an enlargement of the right eye area of the Shroud image. The eye area enlargement shows shadowy outlines of a staff, Greek letters at upper left, and the angle of the side of the coin at upper right. If the objects on the man's eyes are leptons, this not only dates the Shroud to the first century, but also suggests that the process that formed the image acted on inanimate objects as well as on flesh.

7

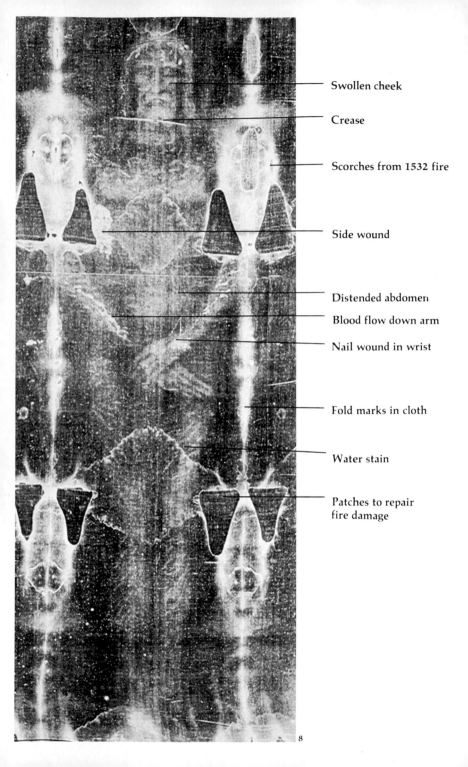

Swollen cheek

Crease

Scorches from 1532 fire

Side wound

Distended abdomen

Blood flow down arm

Nail wound in wrist

Fold marks in cloth

Water stain

Patches to repair
fire damage

8

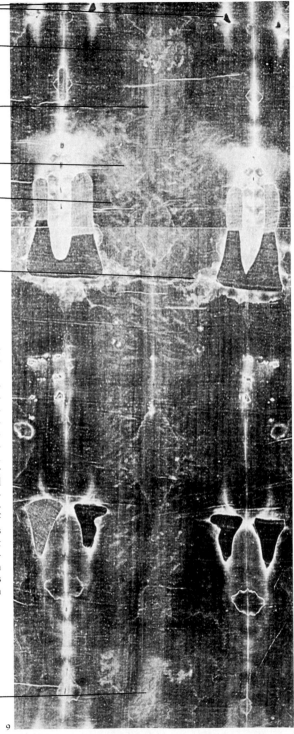

Holes from fire (date unknown)

Blood from scalp punctures

Pigtail

Shoulder abrasions

Scourge wounds

Blood from side wound

These enhanced photographic negatives, taken in 1978, show clear detail on the Shroud image. The nail wounds in the wrist and feet indicate that the man was crucified, and his distended abdomen was probably caused by asphyxiation—the cause of death in crucifixion. The scalp punctures, scourge wounds, shoulder chafing, and side wound—all visible on the image—are consistent with additional punishments inflicted on Jesus of Nazareth. The Shroud was damaged in two fires, but the image was virtually untouched. It is also marked with fold creases and with stains from water used to extinguish one of the fires.

Nail wound in foot

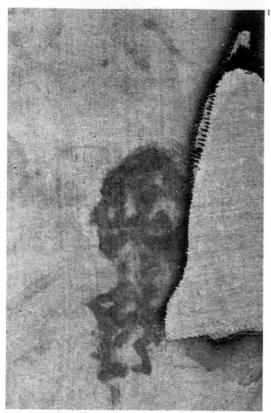

The bloodstains on the Shroud are really blood, the 1978 testing showed. A photo of the side wound taken under ultraviolet light **(left)** shows a thin fluorescent margin around the wound. Dried whole blood does not fluoresce, but blood serum does. The margin is probably serum, a colorless substance which separates from whole blood when it clots. Other studies found that the bloodstain areas contain porphryin, a component of blood. A color photo of the wrist wound **(below)** shows that the man of the Shroud was nailed through the wrists. Blood flowed from this wound in two directions, corresponding to the two positions a crucifixion victim would take on the cross. The absence of thumbs in the image is explained by a little-known fact of anatomy. A nail driven through the wrist in the spot indicated by the image would touch or sever the median nerve, causing the thumbs to curl tightly to the hand.

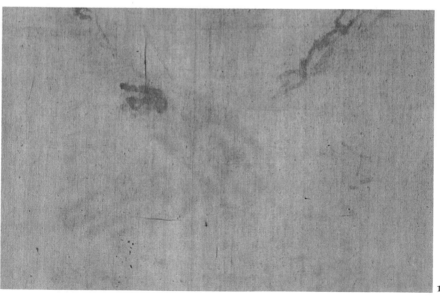

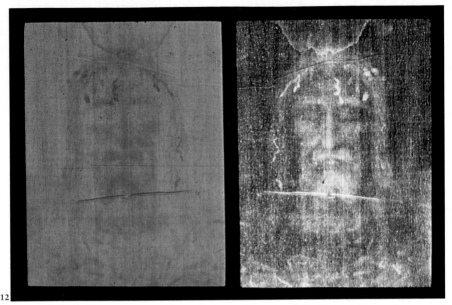

Signs of a brutal beating are visible on the face of the man of the Shroud. The eyebrows and cheeks are swollen, his nose may be broken, and blood flowed from puncture wounds in the scalp. The blood is readily visible on a color photo of the Shroud as you would see it **(left)**. Other details are more distinct on a black-and-white photographic negative of the face **(right)**.

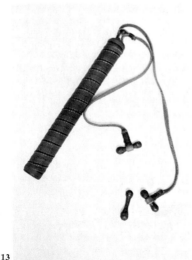

Before crucifixion, Romans repeatedly whipped the man of the Shroud with a flagrum. The dumbbell-shaped pieces of lead on this instrument ripped out pieces of the victim's flesh.

Giovanni Battista della Rovere, a sixteenth-century artist, imagined how the Shroud would have been draped in order to achieve front and back images.

15

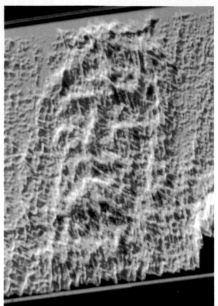

16

17

Space-age technology unlocked the secrets of the Shroud in the 1970s. Scientists discovered that the density of the image varies according to the distance between the cloth and the parts of the body underneath it. Because this relationship can be precisely described mathematically, they were able to create a three-dimensional image of the man buried in the Shroud. The face image **(above right)** shows the objects on the man's eyes which many believe to be coins. The beard is turned up, indicating that a chin band may have been tied around his head to keep his jaw closed in death. The three-dimensional front image **(above left)** shows the swollen abdomen which is the sign of asphyxiation—the cause of death in crucifixion.

Objects over the eyes stand out prominently in a scientific photo **(left)** produced by an advanced photographic process called isodensity. The process enhances subtle details by highlighting differences in the density of the image.

18

Digitised computer photo reveals details in the Shroud image that cannot be seen by the eye or with conventional photography. The digital process, developed to interpret planetary and stellar photographs, uses a microdensitometer to convert differences in image intensity into digital numbers. A computer then reads these numbers and reassembles the photo, highlighting details of interest by assigning arbitrary colors to them. The photo above highlights bloodstains. All details in red have the same spectral features as the side wound.

Subtle blues and striking yellows in the computer-enhanced photo **(right)** make the body image look more realistic. Scientists used an analog computer to remove many non-body details from the picture. Yellow indicates areas of greatest intensity—parts of the body which touched the cloth or which were in contact with it the longest. The shades of blue denote areas of lesser intensity. The photomicrographs **(above)** are among the most important taken during the 1978 testing. The top photo, a closeup of an image area, shows that the image is composed of tiny linen fibrils which are discolored yellow in contrast to the whiter threads of the Shroud itself. The photo beneath is taken from an area containing both bloodstains and image. These photos show that the image is superficial—that is, the yellow fibrils are on the topmost layers of the cloth. The blood seeped into the crevices of the fibers, while the image nowhere penetrated the fabric. Microscopic examination did not find any pigment on the cloth. Scientists have concluded that the Shroud image is not a painting.

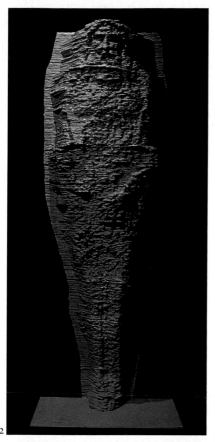

22

Scientists are intrigued by the mystifying and unique properties of the Shroud image. The image's three-dimensional quality is so precise that scientists have been able to construct a cardboard and fiberglass statue of the man buried in the cloth **(left)**. In 1976, scientists at the Jet Propulsion Laboratory used a computer to search the face area for the tell-tale signs of an artist's hand at work. The picture they received **(lower left)** showed that the image is directionless—that is, it came from the body underneath and not from a brush moving from side to side. Close inspection reveals that the image is not affected by heat or water. In the chest area **(below)**, fire scorches, water stains, and the image lie close together. Yet the heat of the fire did not char the image and water did not cause it to run. Some scientists believe that the image is a scorch.

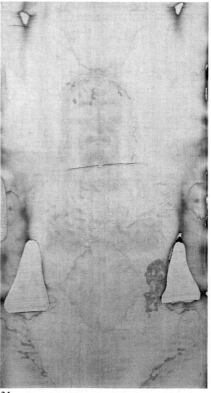

23

24

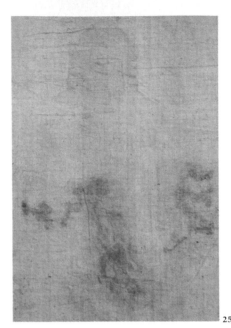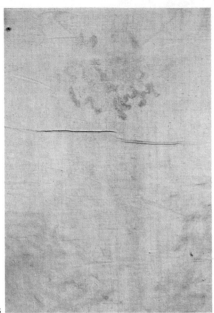

25 26

Ultraviolet photos reveal puzzling details of the bloodstains. The photo of the feet wounds **(above left)** suggests that two nails may have been driven through the man's feet to hold him to the cross. The photo seems to show one wound in the ball of the left foot, another in the heel. Head and back wounds **(above right)** indicate that the man suffered a savage scourging before crucifixion, and that his scalp was punctured by sharp objects—possibly a cap of thorns. Until recently, it was thought that the abrasions visible on the man's shoulders were caused by the rubbing of a heavy object such as a crossbeam. A new theory suggests that they may have been chafed by pressure as his body lay on the hard slab of the tomb. Samuel Pellicori **(below)**, a scientist at the Santa Barbara Research Institute, examines the face of the Shroud image during the 1978 testing.

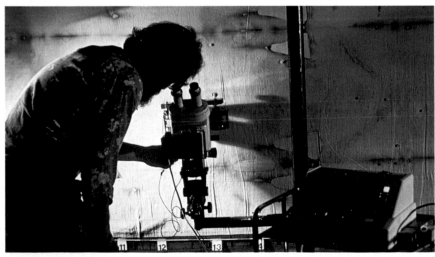

27

28

A truckload of scientific instruments arrives at the Renaissance palace of the Savoys in Turin a few days before the testing began on October 8, 1978. Scientists shipped 72 crates containing sophisticated equipment from the United States for the most extensive examination of an ancient artifact ever conducted.

29

John Jackson, an Air Force physicist and leader of the Shroud of Turin Research Project, briefs team members on the testing schedule before the arrival of the Shroud. Behind him is a specially constructed table designed to hold the Shroud without damage during the testing. The team members studied the Shroud on their own time. Some of their expenses in Turin were met by private donations.

30

31

John Heller of the New England Institute and Joan Janney of the Los Alamos National Scientific Laboratory, examine slides containing Shroud fibers during an evaluation of the Shroud's chemistry.

Robert W. Mottern (left) and Ronald London study a radiograph of the Shroud. X-rays would have detected any pigment on the cloth, but no foreign material that could account for the image was found.

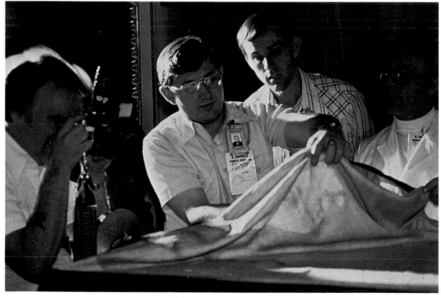

32

The back of the Shroud is inspected for the first time in 400 years. Scientists could see no trace of the image on the underside of the Shroud, confirming the conclusion that the image does not penetrate beyond the topmost threads. Scientists from left are Vernon Miller, Brooks Institute of Photography, Eric Jumper and John Jackson, and Giovanni Riggi of Turin.

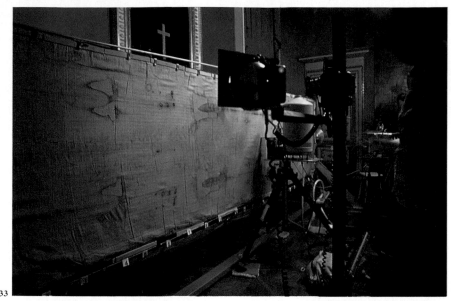

33

Team members stand back during ultraviolet fluorescence photography. During the five days of testing, scientists examined the Shroud across the electromagnetic spectrum with infrared, visible light, ultraviolet, and X-ray radiation.

34

Robert W. Mottern of Sandia Laboratories measures the height of an X-ray source in preparation for an experiment. Mottern was one of the scientists who discovered the three-dimensional property of the image.

35

Vernon Miller of the Brooks Institute of Photography collects data for a spectographic analysis of the Shroud. Miller and his associates took hundreds of photographs of the cloth, including most of those published here.

A likeness of Jesus based on the face of the Shroud of Turin. Painted in 1935 by the Armenian artist Aggemian.

Part II

Conclusions from the Facts

SEVEN

Fraud and the Shroud

SINCE THE BEGINNING OF the Shroud's documented historical existence, many people have doubted that it is genuine. Because the image on the cloth is so remarkable, the question of fraud inevitably arises. Herbert Thurston, the British Jesuit who doubted the authenticity of the Shroud at the turn of the century, put the issue plainly. "If this is not the impression of Christ," he said of the Shroud image, "it was designed as the counterfeit of that impression. In no other person since the world began could these details be verified."[1]

Could this remarkable image be a forgery? Many churchmen in the fourteenth century thought it was. It simply seemed too implausible to believe that Jesus' burial garment had survived, not to speak of the incredible idea that it had been miraculously imprinted with an image of his dead and crucified body. It was only in the twentieth century, with the invention of modern scientific instruments and analytic techniques, that thoughtful people began to seriously entertain the notion that the Shroud might really be authentic.

As we have seen so far in this book, it is extremely difficult to imagine that some clever artist, no matter how skilled, painted the Shroud in the fourteenth century. If the Shroud image is a painting, it departs in dramatic ways from the traditions of medieval Christian art. More importantly, it reveals a degree of anatomical and medical knowledge that no one in the fourteenth century possessed. Moreover, the New Testament argues for the Shroud's authenticity: the Shroud image is consistent with the gospel accounts of Jesus' death and burial. It is also consistent with what is known about Roman crucifixion practices and Jewish burial customs. Then there is the remarkable nature of the image itself. The image is unique. It is a negative, best seen "printed" on a piece of photographic film in the back of a camera, and it also contains three-dimensional and other unusual scientific properties.

The Shroud image seems so incredible that one might say that the burden of proof rests on those who think it is a forgery. Yet the fact that the astonishing qualities of this linen cloth have no complete scientific explanation demands that we explicitly consider the question of fraud.

The fraud charges come from three sources. First, history records a serious accusation of fraud made to the pope in 1389. A bishop claimed that the image was a painting. Second, one scientist has gained some publicity for his recent charge that the Shroud may have been artificially created, a charge that scientists on the Shroud of Turin Research Project dismiss. Third, some have made claims that they can reproduce the Shroud image. We will deal with these issues in this chapter. A fourth issue—the question of spiritual fraud—will be dealt with in Chapter Thirteen.

History: The D'Arcis Memorandum

The Shroud was thought to be a forgery at the very beginning of its documented historical existence. When it was first exhibited in Lirey, France, in 1357, Henri of Poitiers, bishop of Troyes, ordered the exhibition of the relic stopped. History does not record why, but the bishop undoubtedly could not believe that Geoffrey de Charny, a noble knight of modest means, could have somehow acquired the authentic burial shroud of Jesus Christ.

This was only the prelude to an ecclesiastical *cause celebre* thirty-two years later. When the exhibitions resumed in 1389, Henri's successor at Troyes, Bishop Pierre D'Arcis, wrote an angry letter to Pope Clement VII insisting that the relic's exhibition be stopped. His letter to the pope contained a damning charge: Bishop Henri, D'Arcis said, had investigated the Shroud at the time of its first exhibition in 1357 and determined that it was a forgery. He even found the artist who admitted painting it.

For centuries, scholars have regarded the so-called "D'Arcis Memorandum" as proof that the Shroud was a painting. Why would the burial shroud of Jesus Christ appear in provincial France after 1350 years? Relics were often forged and copied in the Middle Ages, and great abuses were connected with the buying and selling of relics, as anyone with the slightest acquaintance with the history of the Christian church must know. Historians regarded the D'Arcis Memorandum as the evidence that the Shroud of Turin was another of these bogus relics. Even in 1902, after the publication of the sensational Secondo Pia photographs, the learned English Jesuit Herbert Thurston dismissed the Shroud in an article in the *Catholic Encyclopedia*.[2] Thurston's opinion was identical with that of Ulysse Chevalier, an eminent French medievalist who dismissed the Shroud in a series of learned studies between 1899 and 1903. Both Thurston and Chevalier based their conclusions on the letter from Pierre D'Arcis to Pope Clement VII in 1389.

It is, therefore, imperative to carefully examine the D'Arcis Memorandum. Why did D'Arcis say what he did?

The historical background to the D'Arcis Memorandum explains much about it.[3] After Bishop Henri of Poitiers ordered the first exhibition of the Shroud stopped in 1357, Jeanne de Vergy, widow of Geoffrey de Charny, waited some thirty years before attempting to display the Shroud again. She remarried, and her husband was the uncle of Pope Clement VII. Clement, who reigned in Avignon during the Western schism, was in a position to be helpful to Jeanne de Vergy, his uncle's wife. Perhaps there was a private "understanding" between the pope and Jeanne to help her exhibit the Shroud once more, and establish its authenticity.

Was this the case? Two historical facts about the second exhibition of the Shroud are undisputed. First, Jeanne and her son, Geoffrey II de Charny, made preparations for the second exhibition quietly. Second they obtained permission for the exhibition directly from the pope, bypassing Pierre D'Arcis, bishop of the diocese where Lirey was located.

The opening of the exhibition in April, 1389 provoked an uproar that eventually involved the pope and the king of France. Bishop D'Arcis, offended by the slight to his authority and perhaps shocked by the size of the crowds which came to view what was called only a "representation" of the true Shroud, immediately ordered the exhibition stopped. The clergy of Lirey appealed to Pope Clement VII and continued the exhibition. The pope confirmed his permission to allow the Shroud to be exhibited and imposed "eternal silence" on Bishop D'Arcis with regard to the subject of the Shroud.

Bishop D'Arcis did not fall silent. He complained to King Charles VI of France, who had also assented to the exhibition. The king withdrew his permission and sent a bailiff to Lirey to seize the Shroud in the name of the crown. The clergy and townspeople refused to surrender the relic. At this point, Bishop D'Arcis wrote his famous memorandum to the pope, including the charge that Bishop Henri had determined that the Shroud was a forgery. He made the charge in the following passage:

The Lord Henry of Poitiers, of pious memory, then Bishop of Troyes, becoming aware of this, and urged by many prudent persons to take action, as indeed was his duty in the exercise of his ordinary jurisdiction, set himself earnestly to work to fathom the truth of this matter. For many theologians and other wise persons declared that this could not be the real shroud of our Lord, having the Saviour's likeness thus imprinted upon it, since the Holy Gospel made no mention of any such imprint while, if it had been true, it was quite unlikely that the holy Evangelists would have omitted to record it, or that the fact should have remained hidden until the present time. Eventually, after diligent inquiry and examination, he discovered the fraud and how said cloth had been cunningly painted, the truth being attested by the artist who had painted it; to wit, that it was a work of human skill and not miraculously wrought or bestowed. Accordingly, after taking mature counsel with wise theologians and men of the law, seeing that he neither ought nor could allow the matter to pass, he began to institute formal proceedings against the said Dean and his accomplices in order to root out this false persuasion. They, seeing their wickedness discovered, hid away the said cloth so that the Ordinary could not find it, and they kept it hidden afterwards for thirty-four years or thereabouts down to the present year [1389].[4]

Bishop D'Arcis' charge that the Shroud had been "cunningly painted" should be taken seriously, but there is good reason to be skeptical about it. The bishop was outraged when he wrote his letter to the pope. The de Charny family and the Lirey clergy had challenged his authority in the diocese. Worse, their challenge had succeeded. They had obtained permission for the exhibition directly from the pope, had defied Bishop D'Arcis' order to stop it, and had even successfully defied the king of France. There may well have been abuses connected with the relic's exposition. After all, the Shroud was officially called only a "representation" of the true burial garment of Jesus, but the peasant faithful were revering it as the authentic Shroud. Bishop D'Arcis had good reason to be angry.

In addition, there are weaknesses in D'Arcis' charges. The most serious is that he produced no evidence that the Shroud was a painting. There is no record that Bishop Henri de Poitiers conducted an investigation into the authenticity of the Shroud. D'Arcis himself produces no such evidence in his letter to the pope. He does not specify when such an investigation was conducted, who conducted it, or the name of the forger who painted the cloth. D'Arcis' successor at Troyes,

Bishop Louis Raguier, maintained that the Shroud was genuine. Furthermore, Henri de Poitiers, the man who was supposed to have determined that the Shroud was a fake, seems to have been on friendly terms with the de Charny family. Pope Clement's response to D'Arcis' letter also casts doubt on the forgery charge. One would expect that the pope would have quickly investigated such an accusation made by a respected bishop. Yet the pope told D'Arcis to keep silent on the subject of the Shroud under penalty of excommunication, and he allowed the exposition at Lirey to continue.[5]

In his rage, D'Arcis may have departed from the literal facts. The forgery charge was very possibly a fiction, but something the bishop was convinced was true. He passed it on to the pope. But there is no evidence that Bishop Henri of Poitiers had ever conducted the investigation as D'Arcis said.

Ian Wilson suggests a more charitable explanation. D'Arcis, he says, could have been referring to a copy of the de Charny Shroud. Many fake shrouds were floating around Europe at the time. Historians count more than forty "true shrouds" in existence during the Middle Ages. Some of them still exist and they are obviously copies of the Lirey cloth. Artists unquestionably *did* copy it. Questions of authenticity did not occur to the unsophisticated popular religious mind of that time as often as they do to us. Simple believers in the fourteenth century would not have been inclined to question the authenticity of a relic whose exposition bore the sanction of the pope. Indeed, this is the substance of Bishop D'Arcis' charges. He told the pope that venal and unscrupulous men had tricked him into sanctioning the exposition of a fraudulent relic. It is thus highly significant that Pope Clement did not investigate, but rather silenced D'Arcis and allowed the expositions of the Shroud to continue.

On the surface, the D'Arcis Memorandum seems impressive. Under the weight of the facts, it begins to collapse. The decisive refutation of D'Arcis' accusations comes from modern science. If the Shroud was painted, the forger's work cannot be detected by skeptics using the most sophisticated analytical technology of the twentieth century.

The Scientific Evidence

When considering the possibility of a forgery in the classic sense of the word, science can investigate several areas. First, are there signs of pigments, dyes, stains, powders, acids, or other artificial or natural colorants on the cloth? Second, is there evidence for the presence of a medium to apply said pigment? Third, are there any signs of an artist's hand at work—brush strokes, block prints, or finger rubbings? Finally, can a duplicate be made of the Shroud image that demonstrates *all* of the known characteristics of the image and still fall within the technological ability of a forger who lived between the first and fourteenth centuries?

We have already discussed the 1978 scientific findings. Let us review the project team's conclusions about forgery.

The answer to the first two questions above—the presence of pigment and medium—is negative. Meticulous testing failed to find any evidence of pigment, powder, dyes, acids or any known colorant or medium to apply it. The image is composed of yellowed linen fibrils. No colorant known in the fourteenth century or today can account for the fibrils. The amount of yellow does not increase in the darker image areas, as would be expected if the image had been painted. Instead, the *density* of the image increases: there are simply more yellowed fibrils present in the darker areas. This characteristic explains why the image is so faint and diffuse, especially at close range.

Scientists have considered—and rejected—other painting theories as well. If a pigment had been applied to the cloth and later cracked off, its residue would be detectable. No residue was found. Neither is there evidence of a medium to apply such a pigment. In fact, it is difficult to see how any kind of medium could have been applied. The image is on the surface fibrils only (to a depth of microns) and in no way soaks through the fibers. This would eliminate any pigment medium applied as a fluid; a fluid would have penetrated and travelled along the fibers, and its presence would have been detected.

Walter McCrone, a microscopist who did not examine the

Shroud in 1978, but who obtained some "sticky tape" samples of cloth material from a member of the Shroud of Turin Research Project, detected the presence of iron oxide on the cloth. He speculates that an artist could have applied a small amount of this material to the linen in order to enhance an already existing image, or perhaps to create the entire image. Members of the Shroud of Turin Research Project regard McCrone's speculations as virtually impossible. They point out that the amount of iron oxide on the Shroud is very minute. The 1978 examination of the cloth did not discover a concentration of iron anywhere near large enough to account for the image. Also, the iron oxide is the wrong color—the image fibrils are yellow, while iron oxide is red.

The most likely explanation for the presence of iron oxide on the cloth is that it originally resided in the red bloodstain areas. The iron was originally abraded blood matter that was transferred to other areas of the cloth as it was folded and unfolded throughout the centuries. The build-up of iron oxide on certain threads could be caused by ceremonial washing and brushing of the Shroud when it was removed from and replaced in its reliquary. Even so, those threads which show a larger than normal concentration of iron are not all in the image areas and are not characteristic of threads in the image areas.

Briefly stated, the investigating scientists specifically tested McCrone's thesis with sophisticated microchemical tests and found that iron oxide cannot account for the Shroud image. Also, submicron iron oxide has been available only within the last two hundred years, thereby meaning that it could not have been used on the Shroud image. Thus it is not surprising that McCrone's research has not been independently verified.

A computer analysis at the Jet Propulsion Laboratory in Pasadena, California adds another piece of evidence against the painting theory—such as McCrone's suggestion. This analysis of the cloth found no directionality in image areas other than the vertical and horizontal patterns of the threads themselves. That meant there was no sign of brush strokes, finger strokes or other methods of artificial application. Even when the computer removed the vertical and horizontal patterns of the fabric weave from the photograph, the image was in essence untouched. In short, there is no evidence of a forger's methods, mediums, or pigments.

Even the Shroud's history belies any painting. The fire of 1532 would have discolored a painting by burning the pigment in some places. The water which extinguished the fire would have caused the image to "run." Neither happened.

However, the facts which best refute hypotheses of fraud (including McCrone's) are the three-dimensional and superficial nature of the image, as well as the absence of any plateaus or saturation points on the image. In short, the scientific analysis has disproved the thesis that the Shroud's image is a painting of any sort.

Modern Attempts at Forgery

It remains then for the skeptic to demonstrate how the cloth could possibly have been forged. The best-known effort to do this has been made by a magician and self-professed amateur detective named Joe Nickell. Nickell has gained some publicity with his theory of how the Shroud was forged.[6] But does the theory match the facts?

Nickell says the Shroud image was created by a dry powdered form of myrrh and aloes brushed onto a cloth stretched over a bas-relief. As evidence he submits photographs of a rubbing obtained from a bas-relief of Bing Crosby which reflects a negative and positive image, but severely degraded in appearance.

The 1973 Italian Commission reported the presence of "granules and globules" of material on the Shroud; the Italians did not identify this material. Nickell says they are the myrrh and aloes his theory requires. However, the Italians denied that these granules and globules are myrrh and aloes and more importantly, reported that they have *nothing whatever to do with the image itself* and are merely particulate matter. Since Nickell's technique requires the build-up of particles in the image area, and since microscopic inspection finds no evidence for this, Nickell's theory seems impossible.

Nickell's faces also fail on aesthetic grounds. They show none of the clarity and resolution of the image on the Turin cloth. Nickell's *Popular Photography* article in which he proposed his theory also contained a lengthy and inaccurate attack on previous research and the work of the Shroud of Turin Research Project. He misquotes or quotes out of context from the *1977 Proceedings* no fewer than eight times, contradicts himself, and reports incorrectly that there is no evidence of blood. (See Appendix A.) Nickell also incorrectly states that the scientists and their predecessors had no direct access to the cloth. This, he claims, is why the investigators found no pigment on the cloth.

The Nickell theory fails for other reasons as well. The fire and water of the 1532 fire would have affected an image formed with organic substances. Photomicrographs reveal that there is no way for an image created by Nickell's method to be superficial in nature. Nickell's "myrrh and aloes" would appear as any particulate would, thereby meaning that his image would not be superficial. Nickell's application of powders would also have a directional nature, but the Shroud image is nondirectional. Additionally, Nickell's theory has difficult problems when aligned against historical facts. What sculptor could have created the masterful bas-relief needed to forge the Shroud according to his method? There is no record or tradition of sculpture to this degree of stark anatomical realism in mid-fourteenth-century France. Moreover, Nickell's technique is not known to have been used before the nineteenth century.

Most devastating to Nickell's hypothesis are the results of testing his image for three-dimensionality on the VP-8 image analyzer. It was found that his image was not three-dimensional. He thus failed to match this crucial feature of the Shroud.

Nickell's attempt to copy the Shroud image is only the latest of many unsuccessful attempts to reproduce it. Painters copied the Shroud in the Middle Ages, but none of these painted shrouds even approach the quality of the original. All were recognized as copies at the time.

This raises an interesting point which further bolsters the case against forgery. Relics were an important part of the popular spirituality of the Middle Ages. Those who flocked to see them were not as troubled by questions of authenticity as we are today. This situation invited the creation of obvious fakes, although the word used at the time was "copies," and this artistic activity did not necessarily carry the connotation of fraudulent intent. An artist who was good enough to create an image as impressive as the Shroud's would surely have made many copies of it. Shroud copies of this level of artistry would have demanded a king's ransom. Where is the statue or the bas-relief that the artist used? It would have graced the finest cathedral and become a famous image in its own right. And, to repeat a point made before, this artist would have had to have forged an image that would not have been appreciated for hundreds of years after his death, until the invention of photography and other modern analytical techniques.

The basic fact remains: neither Joe Nickell nor any other artist or forger has ever created an image showing all the characteristics of the image of the man of the Shroud. For example, none of them are three-dimensional, superficial, or non-directional.

Photographers claim that it is impossible to fake such a delicate image photographically. One cited by Wilcox wrote, "I've been involved in the invention of many complicated processes, and I can tell you that no one could have faked that image. No one could do it today with all the technology we have. It's a perfect negative. It has a photographic quality that is extremely precise."[7] In recent years a skeptical artist and photographer from Great Britain set out to deliberately duplicate the Shroud image using modern photographic techniques. He was convinced at the outset that the Turin cloth was a hoax. In the end, although his results were good enough to be used in the movie, "The Silent Witness," his image is vastly inferior to the original. He concluded that it was virtually impossible for a human to have forged the Shroud image. In fact, the Shroud has never been successfully duplicated even with the aid of modern technology, despite some valiant attempts.

In summary, it is virtually impossible that the Shroud image can be a forgery. The only piece of evidence for fraud is the D'Arcis Memorandum. However, this letter is only an accusation; it contains no evidence, and it may even refer to a copy of the Shroud of Turin. The scientific testing of the Shroud uncovered no evidence for forgery. The technical demands of such a forgery appear far beyond the capabilities of a medieval artist, and modern-day attempts to duplicate the Shroud image have all failed. (See Appendix A.)

We are thus left with three possible conclusions about the origin of the image of the man buried in the Shroud of Turin. Let us review them.

1. It is a freak occurrence of human genius. Someone forged the image in the fourteenth century or earlier. Twentieth-century science can find no trace of how he did it. He worked in an unknown way, with unknown materials, without the ability to check his work or know his results.

2. It is a freak occurrence of nature. An unknown, but natural chemical process formed the image of a crucifixion victim in a tomb. The way the material was applied to the cloth is also unknown.

3. The image is a record of a known man—Jesus of Nazareth— at a known moment in history. The image is probably a scorch. How this happened is not known now and may never be known in scientific terms—because it involved an action of God outside the laws of nature.

We can rule out the first possible conclusion. We can have confidence that modern science could detect the work of a forger. The report of the Shroud of Turin Research Project did not seriously consider the possibility that the third possible conclusion is the most likely, since science is not equipped to deal with such issues. Nevertheless, it does seem to be the most logical, and it is not good science to refuse to consider it on the grounds that "mechanism" for a scorch is not "technologically credible." (See Chapters Eleven and Twelve.)

Nevertheless, even the second conclusion points inescapably to the probability that the Shroud is authentic. This is the question we take up now.

EIGHT

The Authenticity
of the Shroud

WE ARE NOW IN a position to try to reach a verdict on the Shroud. The Shroud of Turin is reputed to be the burial garment of Jesus Christ. Is the evidence for this claim persuasive? Is the Shroud authentic? Is it really Jesus' burial garment? Is the image of the man buried in the Shroud an image of Jesus Christ? We will answer these questions in the next two chapters.

The scientific and historical data presented so far in this book has not decisively shown that the image on the Turin Shroud is that of Jesus, but our study of the scientific and historical data attests that the Shroud is at least authentic and not a forgery.

Human craft did not create the image on the Shroud. Scientists are convinced that the cloth once held a dead body, which left an image of itself. It is most likely that the image was caused by some kind of a scorch process. The bloodstains on the cloth are really blood. Although the historical record of the cloth is incomplete and it has not been scientifically dated to the time of Jesus, however, historical data such as the material type, the coins over the eyes, the presence of pollen from the

Middle East point to a probable first-century origin.

However, this scientific and historical evidence, fascinating and suggestive though it is, cannot tell us everything we want to know about the Shroud of Turin. It cannot, for example, tell us whether the man of the Shroud is Jesus Christ. The firmest conclusion reached by the Shroud of Turin Research Project is that the Shroud is not a painting or a forgery. It is probable that the image is some type of scorch, but the scientists cannot explain how a corpse scorched a linen burial shroud, leaving a detailed image with extraordinary optical properties. This is why some scientists are reluctant to arrive at final conclusions about the Shroud. They want a complete solution to the problem, but a comprehensive *totally scientific* explanation for the Shroud and its image does not exist.

The limitations of science in this matter are even more profound than this. Even if scientists date the Shroud precisely and discover more about the process that produced the image, they will never finally and irrevocably identify the Shroud of Turin as the burial shroud of Jesus Christ. The necessary scientific data about Jesus does not exist independently of the Shroud—a record of Christ's picture, blood type, dental records, finger prints, and so forth. Lacking this, science can never logically foreclose the possibility that someone else besides Jesus suffered the same way he did and that his body left a mysterious record of these sufferings on his burial shroud.

Fortunately, it is still possible to reach a verdict. Physical science is not the only source of evidence. There is history and archaeology. The gospels, ancient documents of demonstrated historical reliability, speak of the sufferings, death, and burial of Jesus of Nazareth. Archaeological data also enables us to verify the historical reliability of the scriptures, crucifixion practices, burial customs, and other aspects of the Shroud. We can then compare the gospel witness to the Shroud image.

We will draw conclusions about the Shroud in two steps. The first question asks whether the Shroud is genuine. Is the Shroud what it appears to be: an ancient burial garment bearing the image of a dead man who suffered a violent death? We will deal further with the question of authenticity in this chapter, building on the scientific consensus that the Shroud is not a fake. (See Chapter Seven.) The second question asks whether the man of the Shroud is Jesus Christ. We will deal with the identity of the man of the Shroud in Chapter Nine.

Archaeology and Scripture

The man of the Shroud can be identified as Jesus Christ only by the use of the scriptural accounts of Jesus' crucifixion, death, and burial. Before we compare the Shroud image to the gospel accounts, we need to ask whether the scripture is historically reliable. The work of archaeologists and other scholars strongly suggests that it is.

Archaeologists have long maintained that archaeological investigation confirms the historicity of the scripture. According to Nelson Glueck, a renowned archaeologist who worked extensively in the Middle East:

> It may be stated categorically that no archaeological discovery has ever controverted a Biblical reference. Scores of archaeological findings have been made which confirm in clear outline or exact detail historical statements in the Bible.[1]

To be sure, questions arise from such discoveries, but as Millar Burrows points out:

> On the whole, however, archaeological work has unquestionably strengthened confidence in the reliability of the scriptural record. More than one archaeologist has found his respect for the Bible increased by the experience of excavation in Palestine.[2]

Other archaeologists say that their discoveries have specifically confirmed the historical accuracy of the biblical texts. William F. Albright explains, "There can be no doubt that archaeology has confirmed the substantial historicity of the Old Testament tradition."[3] Sir Frederick Kenyon concurs, noting that archaeology has served to further establish the authority of the Old Testament, thereby disproving the claims of biblical critics who have attempted to dismiss its trustworthiness.[4]

Kenyon, a former director of the British Museum, points out that modern archaeological research has actually strengthened the reliability of the scriptures by clearing up apparent discrepancies between biblical accounts and other ancient histories. One example concerns the account of the Babylonian king Belshazzar. Daniel 5 says that the Medes and Persians killed Belshazzar when they took the Babylonian Empire. Ancient secular history seems to contradict the Bible. Other documents say that Nabonides was the last king of Babylon, and that he was not killed when the empire fell. Since nothing was known about Belshazzar outside the scriptural mention until the last century, this was an often-cited example of the supposed historical unreliability of scripture.

However, archaeology has vindicated the scriptural record. In the late nineteenth century, Assyriologist Theophilus Pinches studied a large number of clay tablets from ancient Babylon which had been unearthed earlier in the century. They told an unusual story. Not only did the tablets mention Belshazzar, but they connected him to Nabonides and called him the king's son. The Babylonian custom at the time was to make oaths in the name of the current king, and one tablet showed that oaths were sworn in the names of both Nabonides and Belshazzar. Further research by Yale Assyriologist Raymond Dougherty revealed that Nabonides and Belshazzar reigned as "co-kings." In the later portion of his reign, Nabonides spent much time in Arabia, away from Babylon; he entrusted his kingship in Babylon to his son Belshazzar. The Medes and Persians took their kingdom, pensioned off Nabonides, and killed Belshazzar.[5]

Archaeologists have found the Bible to be so accurate that they have used it for guidance in their work. One of the best-known examples is Nelson Glueck's discovery of Solomon's port city of Ezion-geber. Glueck excavated the location mentioned in 1 Kings 9:26 and 10:22 and found the city exactly where the text indicated.[6] When the site of ancient Nineveh was excavated in 1849-1850 by Austen H. Layard, he found that the scriptural description of the glories of the city was indeed historically accurate.[7]

Archaeological and historical research has also supported the historicity of the New Testament. F.F. Bruce, the eminent British scripture scholar and classicist, lists many of these independent confirmations in his book, *The New Testament Documents: Are They Reliable?*[8] These are some of Bruce's examples. The pool of Bethesda, described in the gospel of John, has been located in the northeast corner of the old city of Jerusalem; the excavations uncovered a pool exactly as John described it. At the end of his epistle to the Romans, Paul adds greetings from Erastus, the city treasurer of Corinth; in 1929, archaeologists found a paving stone in the ruins of Corinth listing Erastus as the treasurer of the city. Luke, the author of Acts as well as of his own gospel, consciously wrote as a historian. Modern historians have found him to be extraordinarily accurate, even down to such relatively unimportant details as the exact titles of the various civil authorities in Palestine and the other Middle Eastern areas evangelized by Paul. After reviewing many examples of Luke's historical accuracy, Bruce concludes:

> All these evidences of accuracy are not accidental. A man whose accuracy can be demonstrated in matters where we are able to test it is likely to be accurate even where the means for testing him are not available. Accuracy is a habit of mind, and we know from happy (or unhappy) experiences that some people are habitually accurate just as others can be depended upon to be inaccurate. Luke's record entitles him to be regarded as a writer of habitual accuracy.[9]

These are a few examples of the accuracy of the New Testament. As Bruce also points out, the extant New Testament manuscripts are far closer to the date of the original work than manuscripts of any other ancient classic work. There are also many more ancient copies of the New Testament than any other ancient work. Thus the copying accuracy of the New Testament is probably greater. Also, while many classics such as the histories of Livy and Tacitus have large portions which are now lost, the New Testament is complete. As a historical source, the New Testament is accurate, as is recognized.[10]

It is important to note that archaeology also confirms the accuracy of historical statements in scripture. This accuracy is further supported by historical investigation. When the gospels say that Jesus was crucified and buried in a certain way, there is no reason to doubt the truth of these details on purely historical grounds, especially since manuscript evidence, archaeology and ancient historical sources verify the gospel accounts in these areas, as we shall see.

Archaeology and Crucifixion

Archaeology has a direct bearing on our inquiry into the Shroud's authenticity. One important discovery reveals much about the nature of crucifixion in the first century A.D. In June, 1968, a section of Jerusalem was being excavated in order to prepare for the building of new apartments. The workmen uncovered an ancient Jewish burial ground on the site, about one mile north of the Old Damascus Gate. Archaeologist Vasilius Tzaferis investigated the site and found fifteen stone ossuaries, stone chests used for reburying skeletons after the flesh had decayed.[11] The ossuaries contained the remains of some thirty-five Jews who died in the revolt against Rome about 70 A.D. Some of these Jews had suffered violent deaths; one child had been killed by an arrow and two persons had been burned to death. Three other children had died of starvation and an elderly woman had been beaten to death.

One skeleton was of a man who had been crucified. His name, written in Aramaic on the ossuary in which he was buried, was Yohanan Ben Ha'galgol. Yohanan was about 5'7" tall, was 24-28 years old, and had a cleft palate. A seven-inch nail, still intact, had been driven through his heel bones. This meant that his feet and legs had been twisted sideways to be nailed to the cross. The nail first went through a plaque or wedge made from acacia wood, through the heels, and into the vertical beam of the cross. Splinters on the spike indicated that the cross had been made of olive wood. The end of the nail was bent, either purposely or by a knot in the wood.

An Israeli pathologist, Dr. Nicu Haas of Jerusalem's Hebrew University, examined Yohanan's skeleton.[12] He found that nails had also been driven just above Yohanan's wrists between the radius and ulna bones. The radius bone at this point was not only scratched, but was worn smooth, probably by constant and gradual friction as Yohanan continually pulled himself up to breathe and then sank back down again.

Haas also found that Yohanan's calf bones were broken—specifically, his right tibia and left tibia and fibula bones. They seem to have been broken in a single, crushing blow—the Roman *crucifragium*, recorded in John 19:31-32 as being administered to the two thieves on either side of Jesus in order to hasten their deaths. Yohanan's legs were apparently sawed off later in order to separate them from the cross.

Yohanan's skeleton is another outstanding example of how archaeology has backed up the scripture. Specifically, it verifies the gospel accounts of the details of crucifixion. Victims were nailed to their crosses through the feet or heels and through the wrists. Executioners smashed the ankle bones of those who did not die within a certain time, as with the thieves crucified on each side of Jesus. The ancient Roman historian Tacitus also records some of these same details concerning crucifixion, providing further confirmation.[13] These are examples of the reasons why we can regard as trustworthy the scriptural accounts of Jesus' crucifixion and burial.

Archaeology and the Shroud

In Section I we answered various questions concerning the authenticity of the Shroud. It was found that scientific testing, especially since October, 1978, has vindicated the authentic nature of this artifact. It can be shown that the image on the Shroud was not the result of paint, dye, powder, acid, or other substances being added to the linen material. Neither was the image caused by direct contact with any foreign substance. Therefore, no fakery was involved. Even though they would entail natural processes, it was also found that the diffusion of vapors and natural contact theories probably cannot account for the formation of the image.

It may thus be concluded that the Shroud is an authentic archaeological artifact. Whether it wrapped the body of Jesus and if it may relate anything concerning his death and resurrection is still to be determined. However, the scientists who investigated the Shroud, even those who are skeptics and agnostics, agree that it is an authentic archaeological find. Such a conclusion is very probable and is demanded by the weight of the evidence.

At this point, we should examine the Shroud as an archaeologist would. Can the anthropological and archaeological data further identify the man of the Shroud and help determine that it is indeed authentic?

Experts agree that facial features identify the man buried in the Shroud as a Caucasian. Carlton Coon, a leading ethnologist, says he has the physical features of a Jew or Arab.[14] The man's hairstyle, characterized by a beard and long hair parted in the middle, further identifies him as a Jew. In addition, the hair in back is cut in the form of a pigtail, a hairstyle very common for first-century Jewish men.[15] It is thus probable that this crucified person was a Jew.

His executioners were most probably Romans. A close study of the wounds inflicted by whipping reveals that the instrument used had multiple thongs, each having a dumbbell-shaped piece of metal or bone on the end. Each blow from the scourge would therefore cause several lacerations on the skin. Such an instrument, called the *flagrum*, is known to have been used by Romans in the first few centuries A.D. This much-feared whip utilized pieces of metal or bone on the end of the thongs in order to gouge out pieces of the victim's flesh. It was used in the martyrdom of Christians in the Roman Empire. The *flagrum* is depicted on ancient Roman coins, and an actual specimen was found in the Roman city of Herculaneum. Since the *flagrum* was commonly employed by Romans but not by other ancient peoples, this is archaeological evidence that the man buried in the Shroud was beaten by Romans.[16] The extensive beating itself indicates that the man of the Shroud was not a

Roman citizen. Roman citizens were not beaten so severely, and never with a *flagrum*.

There are also additional indications that the man buried in the Shroud was executed by Romans. The Romans often used crucifixion for capital punishment.[17] The skeleton of Yohanan further identifies the man of the Shroud as a victim of Roman crucifixion. Both the man buried in the Shroud and Yohanan were nailed through the wrists. Both men were also nailed through the feet, with the man in the Shroud being nailed through the top of the feet while Yohanan was nailed sideways through the heel bones. Yohanan's ankle bones were smashed in order to hasten his death, while the man of the Shroud's legs were not broken. Yet the spear wound in the man's side must have served virtually the same purpose—to make sure that he was dead and not simply faking. This spear wound is another indication that Romans were involved in the man's execution. The wound inflicted in the side of the man in the Shroud measures 1¾ inches by 7/16 inch. This opening exactly corresponds to the size of the tip of the *lancia*, a Roman spear with a long, thin, leaf-shaped head.[18]

Additional archaeological confirmation comes from recent discoveries about Jewish burial practices. In the late 1970s, archaeologists excavated an ancient Jewish cemetery in the hill country surrounding Jericho. This large cemetery was used from the first century B.C. until the destruction of Jericho in 68 A.D. The archaeologists found many wooden coffins and stone ossuaries; like Yohanan, the names of the deceased persons were sometimes imprinted on the outside of the ossuaries.

The tombs in the cemetery were carved out of rock. They were roughly semi-circular, with horizontal burial chambers ranging like spokes around a center vestibule about six feet in height.[19] Presumably this was high enough to allow a person to stand upright and is therefore an approximate indication of the height of first-century Jews. This confirms our earlier statement that another ancient Jewish gravesite revealed that the average height of adult males buried there was 5 feet, 10 inches. It provides general confirmation of the fact that the man buried in the Shroud, a man approximately 5 feet, 10 inches tall, could have been a first-century Jew.

More specific evidence comes from another discovery from these tombs. Two coins were found in one of the skulls buried in the cemetery. The coins dated from the reign of Herod Agrippa (41-44 A.D.) and had undoubtedly been placed over the eyes of the deceased.[20] This appears to have been a custom in first-century Palestine. Photographs indicate that the man buried in the Shroud had coins placed over his eyes.

Conclusion

This review of relevant archaeological and anthropological data strongly indicates that the Shroud is authentic. There is no reason to doubt that the cloth is anything other than an ancient burial garment imprinted with the image of a real corpse. The archaeological and historical record not only confirms the scientific finding that the Shroud is not a fraud; it provides much positive evidence to help identify the cloth and the man buried in it. The archeological survey indicates that the man was a Jew, crucified by Romans, and buried in general accordance with Jewish burial customs.

One other important point is that this archaeological data shows the Shroud to be consistent with first-century practices and further corroborates a first-century date for the Shroud. Archaeology and the 1978 scientific testing both show that the Shroud is not a forgery, but is rather an authentic archeological artifact. Archaeology also contributes to the question we ask in the next chapter: is the man of the Shroud Jesus Christ? It verifies the historical trustworthiness of the gospels, which speak in some detail about one first-century Jew who was crucified by Romans.

NINE

Is It Jesus?

IS THE MAN BURIED in the Shroud Jesus Christ? We are ready to try to answer this key question.

Scientific testing has established the Shroud's authenticity. The scientists have concluded that the Shroud is very probably a genuine artifact and not a fraud. This conclusion has been reinforced by an examination of relevant archaeological data about Jewish customs.

The scholarly consensus is that the Shroud of Turin is a real burial garment which once held the corpse of a Jew who was crucified by Romans and buried in general accordance with Jewish burial practices. The data points toward first-century Palestine as the likely time and place of his execution and burial, and thus as the date for the cloth as well.

We are thus faced with two alternatives. The man buried in the Shroud was either Jesus Christ, or it was some other victim of crucifixion. This is the choice which the scientific data inevitably gives us.

To determine whether the Shroud of Turin is the burial garment of Jesus, we will examine both alternatives. First, we will review the evidence that Jesus is the man buried in the

Shroud; then we will assess the possibility that the man is someone else.

Jesus and the Shroud

It is revealing to compare the wounds inflicted on the man buried in the Shroud with the witness of the New Testament concerning the crucifixion procedure used with Jesus. The correlation is, simply stated, quite remarkable.

Before he was crucified, Jesus was subjected to a variety of punishments. The Roman soldiers scourged him (Matthew 27:26; Mark 15:15; John 19:1). The man of the Shroud was beaten very severely. Ricci counts more than 220 scourge wounds on his body, located on almost every area with the exception of the head, feet, and arms.[1] Wilson records somewhat fewer scourge wounds, but still enough to constitute a very severe beating.[2] We have seen how these marks were most likely inflicted by the Roman *flagrum*, a feared instrument of torture which inflicted great pain by sometimes even ripping out small pieces of flesh with each blow.

The Romans also mocked Jesus for his claims to be the Son of God and the Messiah. The soldiers placed a purple robe on him and put a reed in his hand in order to jeer him, pretending to address him as king. They even bowed down to him, imitating worship. Then, to further scoff at him, they made a crown out of thorns and forcefully placed it on his head (Matthew 27:29; Mark 15:17-20; John 19:2).

This is another close parallel between Jesus and the man in the Shroud. Numerous puncture wounds can be observed in the man's scalp. Close examination reveals that these wounds differ from those caused by the scourging and were independently inflicted.[3]

The gospels also relate that Jesus was repeatedly struck in the face (Matthew 27:30; Mark 15:19; Luke 22:63-64; John 19:3). Such a beating can be observed in the image on the Shroud. The man has several bruises and swellings around both eyes, both cheeks, the nose, and the chin.

After Jesus' scourging, mock crowning with thorns, and beating, he was taken away to be crucified. He was made to carry his own cross (John 19:17) but apparently stumbled and fell, since a bystander, Simon of Cyrene, was forced to carry it for him (Matthew 27:32; Mark 15:21; Luke 23:26).

Bruises on the upper back just below the shoulders indicate that the man in the Shroud also carried or supported a heavy object. We know this happened *after* the scourging, because the rubbing of the heavy object slightly altered the scourge wounds underneath. Additionally, there are cuts and bruises on both knees, indicating a fall on a hard surface. The left knee is particularly badly cut.

The gospels relate that Jesus was nailed to the cross through the feet and the hand-wrist area (Luke 24:39; John 20:20, 25-27). The Shroud likewise shows a man pierced through the wrists at the base of the palms and through the feet. Forensic pathologists are convinced that the man, like Jesus, was crucified.

A striking similarity concerns the gospel report that normal crucifixion procedure included breaking the legs of the victims in order to hasten death (John 19:31-32). The discovery of the skeleton of Yohanan verifies the gospel report. However, the gospels say that the soldiers did not break Jesus' legs because he was already dead. Instead, a Roman soldier stabbed him in the side in order to assure his death. Blood and water flowed from the open wound (John 19:33-34).

Similarly, the man in the Shroud did not have his legs broken and he was also stabbed in the side. Amazingly, a mixture of blood and water is ascertainable on the Shroud. The blood and water flowed vertically down the right side of the chest to the waist, where it spread horizontally across the back.

Crucifixion was a punishment reserved for slaves, war captives, and the worst political prisoners. Therefore, there was normally very little interest in providing the victim with anything more than a minimal burial. Yet, the gospels explain that Jesus was buried by Joseph of Arimathea, a wealthy man who placed Jesus' body in his own new tomb. Joseph gave Jesus an individual burial, complete with linen wrappings and spices (Matthew 27:57-60; Mark 15:43-46; Luke 23:50-55; John 19:38-42). In spite of this attention and care, the burial process was hurried and was not completed before the Sabbath began (Mark 16:1; Luke 23:55-24:1).

The case of the man in the Shroud is similar. He was also buried individually in linen wrappings and there are also indications that his burial was not completed. (See Chapter Four.)

This comparison of the gospel accounts with the sufferings and burial of the man of the Shroud points to the strong likelihood that the man is Jesus Christ. The evidence is consistent at every point. The man of the Shroud suffered, died, and was buried the way the gospels say Jesus was.

The Alternative: Another Man

Before concluding that the man of the Shroud is Jesus, we must consider the possibility that he is someone else—another Jew tortured and crucified by Romans and buried according to Jewish customs. Science cannot resolve this question, but there is sufficient historical data to make a decision based on probability. We can do this because the crucifixion and burial of Jesus differed significantly from the ordinary ways the Romans crucified criminals and the Jews buried their dead. Jesus' case was irregular. He was scourged, crowned with thorns, nailed to his cross, stabbed in the side (instead of his legs being broken), buried well but incompletely, and his body left the cloth before it decomposed. Because we know a fair amount about Roman and Jewish customs in these matters, we can assess the probability that *two* men were crucified and buried this way. Such a probability, in reverse, would be the probability that the Shroud of Turin is the burial garment of Jesus Christ.

Several Shroud researchers and scientists have already tried to computed such a probability. One is Francis Filas, professor of theology at Loyola University and a long-time investigator of the Shroud. Fr. Filas believes that there is very little chance that the man buried in the Shroud could be someone other than Jesus. Citing the correspondence between the Shroud and the irregularities of Jesus' crucifixion, Fr. Filas computes the total possibility that the man in the Shroud was not Jesus as

1 in 10^{26}, thereby virtually identifying the Shroud as Jesus' burial garment.[4]

A more conservative figure was devised by Vincent J. Donovan. Donovan was also impressed by the ways irregularities in Jesus' crucifixion correspond to the Shroud, especially the crown of thorns, the fact that Jesus' ankles were not broken, the spear wound, and the incomplete burial. Donovan concludes that there is a probability of 1 chance in 282 billion that the person buried in the Shroud was someone other than Jesus.[5]

French Jesuit and engineer Paul de Gail is another scholar who attempted to compute the probability that the Shroud wrapped someone other than Jesus. De Gail arrived at a much higher figure than Donovan's 1 in 282 billion, in spite of the fact that he performed his research in 1972, before some of the most surprising discoveries about the Shroud were made.[6]

The most conservative probability arrived at thus far was computed in 1978 by Professors Tino Zeuli and Bruno Barbaris, two members of the science faculty at the University of Turin. Zeuli and Barbaris combined a skeptical approach with a mastery of statistics. They still concluded that the chances were 1 in 225 billion that someone other than Jesus was buried in the Shroud.[7]

Statistical analyses such as these are not meaningless guesses. They are respectable scientific tools. Scientists employ them continually to weigh the merits of alternative theories to explain observed phenomena. These previous calculations about the Shroud—ranging from 1 in 225 billion to 1 in 10^{26}—virtually identify the Shroud of Turin beyond any reasonable doubt as Jesus' burial garment. We will now make our own calculations. We will deliberately take a skeptical posture, and compute our probability as conservatively as possible.

To keep our figure as low as possible, we will ignore the facts that the person in the Shroud is a crucified man. We will not include the probability that the person is a man and not a woman (1 in 2) and that the person who died was a victim of crucifixion. Donovan very conservatively estimates that one man in 500 died of crucifixion at the time, a figure which is almost certainly much higher.[8] Thus, even before we look at the specifics of Jesus' scourging, crucifixion, and burial, we would already have a probability of 1 in 1000. Again, we will bypass this methodology in the interest of a skeptical approach.

1. Our first fact is Jesus' scourging and other mistreatment at the hands of his executioners. A beating was sometimes administered to those being crucified, but the beating was rarely so serious. The Shroud also depicts a very extensive beating, one which was so severe that it may have eventually caused the man's death.[9] In spite of the rarity of this beating, which both Jesus and the man in the Shroud suffered, we will give only a 1 in 2 probability that a crucified man other than Jesus was beaten this way.

2. It is very unusual that a man to be crucified as a criminal would be crowned with thorns beforehand. Romans participated in formal emperor worship. How likely is it that they would routinely crown condemned criminals and slaves with thorns, and pretend to worship them? Crowning indicates majesty and a crown of thorns would, of course, mock that proclaimed majesty. Jesus was crowned with thorns for this very reason—to mock his claims to be the Son of God and the Messiah, thus the "ruler" of the Jews. The man buried in the Shroud was also pierced throughout the scalp. If the man in the Shroud is not Jesus, what are the chances that this man, probably a criminal or slave, would have been crowned with thorns? By any estimate, this is an improbable occurrence.[10] A conservative guess would be 1 in 500. We will choose a figure of 1 in 400.

3. Many crucifixion victims were tied to their crosses with ropes. Both Jesus and the man buried in the Shroud were nailed. We will estimate the probability that another man was also nailed as 1 in 2.

4. The gospels and archaeological data indicate that the Romans commonly broke the legs of crucified persons in order to hasten their death. Since Jesus was already dead, his legs were not broken. Neither were the man in the Shroud's legs broken. Since leg-breaking was normal procedure, we will estimate the probability of its not occurring as 1 in 3.

5. To insure that Jesus was dead, a soldier stabbed him in the side, and blood and water flowed from the wound. The same

thing happened to the man in the Shroud. Let us consider the probabilities that the same thing happened to some other man. The soldier could have done nothing, used a sword, or used a spear (1 in 3). To insure death, he could have struck the head, stomach, or side (1 in 3). Finally, blood and water flowed from the wound (1 in 3). We are being very skeptical by placing a probability of all of these occurring at 1 in 27.

6. Since most crucified victims were criminals, slaves, and rebels, few were given individual burials in a fine linen shroud. Jesus was buried in linen with spices and placed in a new tomb. The man buried in the Shroud was also wrapped in fine linen and buried individually. We conservatively estimate the probability of a "criminal" being buried this way at 1 in 8.

7. The gospels relate that Jesus had to be buried hastily in order to be placed in the tomb before the Sabbath. Because the process could not be completed in time, the women returned to finish the job on Sunday morning. The man in the Shroud was also buried hastily and the process was incomplete at the time of burial. How many crucified victims receiving individual burials in fine linen shrouds were nevertheless buried hastily? We will conservatively estimate the probability of this happening as 1 in 8.

8. The New Testament asserts that Jesus' body did not undergo corruption (Acts 2:22-32) but that he was raised from the dead. We will consider the question of the historicity of the resurrection in Chapter Eleven. Here we will simply note the parallel with the Shroud. There are no signs of decomposition on the Shroud. Additionally, the bloodstains are anatomically perfect and have not been smeared by the linen being separated from the body.[11] This parallel is especially interesting because we have many ancient burial shrouds showing decomposition stains. Thus we have to estimate the probability that another crucified man's body was somehow removed from its burial shroud before it decomposed, and in such a way that the wounds were not smeared. We will conservatively estimate this probability as being 1 in 10.

The gospels say that these eight irregularities were present in Jesus' death and burial. The Shroud evidence says they were also present in the death and burial of the man of the Shroud. We have estimated the probability that they happened to someone other than Jesus, deliberately using skeptical and conservative estimates. Yet, multiplying these probabilities, we have 1 chance in 82,944,000 that the man buried in the Shroud is not Jesus.

This ratio of nearly 83 million to 1 is almost meaningless to many of us. Yet consider this practical illustration. 82,944,000 dollar bills laid end-to-end would stretch from New York to San Francisco more than three times. Suppose one of these bills is marked, and a blindfolded person is given one chance to find it. The odds that he will succeed are 1 in 82,944,000. These are the odds that the man buried in the Shroud is someone other than Jesus Christ.

There is a chance that the man of the Shroud is someone else, just as there is a chance that the blindfolded person would find the marked bill. But the odds are practically infinitesimal. There is no practical probability that someone other than Jesus Christ was buried in the Shroud of Turin.

Some of the statistical estimates made about the frequency of irregularities in Jesus' death and burial may be open to challenge. We have relatively little data about some aspects of Roman crucifixion. This is why our calculations were deliberately conservative. Indeed, the odds of 82,944,000 to 1 are most likely too low rather than too high. We could have increased the odds a thousandfold by considering the facts that the Shroud image shows a man (not a woman) who was crucified (instead of dying by some other means). Our estimates concerning the chest wound, the frequency of good burials of crucifixion victims, hasty burials in linen, and the absence of decomposition are almost certainly too low. However, even apart from probability studies, a comparison reveals that it is highly likely that the man in the Shroud is Jesus of Nazareth.

There are also two other major points to consider. First, we were conservative in choosing to compare *points in common* between the Shroud and the gospel accounts of Jesus. Our figure would have been much higher if we included the fact that there are no contradictions between the gospel and the

Shroud, an indication of an even closer correspondence. Since there are no contradictions in other aspects, then it is even more probable that the Shroud is the actual linen cloth in which Jesus was buried. Second, an earlier point should be recalled. The Shroud is not a recently discovered artifact that merely reminds us of Jesus. Rather, it has been kept through the centuries as his actual burial garment, even in times when this belief could not be scientifically tested. This further increases the chances that Jesus is the man buried in the Shroud because it produces an even closer correlation. In spite of skeptical procedures, we have a very probable correspondence between these two men.

We tried to estimate probabilities conservatively. Nevertheless, the result still leaves a very high probability that the man buried in the Shroud is Jesus. As Ricci writes, the converging data " . . . will cause us to conclude that the Man of the Shroud is that Jesus of whom the Gospels speak, excluding any other crucified person in history."[12]

Thus we conclude that, according to high probability, the man buried in the Shroud is none other than Jesus. The Shroud of Turin is his actual burial garment. Such a conclusion is very strongly supported by the facts.

Part III

The Significance of the Shroud

TEN

The Death of Jesus: New Insights?

WE HAVE EXAMINED THE evidence and reached a verdict. It is highly probable that the Shroud of Turin is the burial garment which covered Jesus as he lay in the tomb. An image of his body is imprinted on the cloth.

Several independent lines of evidence converge on this conclusion. Scientific investigation determined that the Shroud image is not a forgery, but was created by a real body. The study of art history, ancient textiles, botany, and numismatics indicates that the Shroud has a probable first-century origin. The study of Roman crucifixion procedure and Jewish burial customs indicates that the man buried in the Shroud was probably a Jew crucified by Romans. Our final conclusion that the man is Jesus is based on a study of probabilities. The man of the Shroud's sufferings and burial correspond exactly to Jesus' sufferings and burial, even in areas where these differed from normal Roman and Jewish procedure.

The final four chapters of this book will draw out the further conclusions from the known facts about the Shroud of Turin. This chapter will discuss what the Shroud reveals about the death of Jesus. Chapter Eleven confronts the question of whether the Shroud contains evidence for Jesus' resurrection. Chapter Twelve discusses the implications the Shroud has for the naturalism-supernaturalism debate, and the last chapter draws some final conclusions.

The Shroud and Medical Opinion

The anatomical accuracy of the Shroud image has attracted the attention of many medical experts in the twentieth century. From the beginning of such medical studies, these doctors have been greatly impressed by such features as the exactness of the image, the clear outline of the wounds, the correctness of the flows of blood, its characteristic clotting, and the separation of serum and cellular mass. Paul Vignon, professor of biology at Paris' Institute Catholique, and a leader in this initial research, published a book on the subject in 1902.[1]

Yves Delage, a friend of Vignon and professor of anatomy at the Sorbonne in Paris, also made important studies around the same time. An agnostic and a member of the prestigious French Academy, Delage found that the wounds on the Shroud were anatomically accurate and that there were no traces of fraud. He concluded that it was highly probable that it was the burial garment of Jesus.[2]

Some of the most detailed medical studies were done by Pierre Barbet, an eminent surgeon at St. Joseph's Hospital in Paris. He used cadavers for experiments on crucifixion and found that this research corroborated the 'authenticity of the Shroud. Barbet also studied the lance wound in Jesus' side, and concluded that this object passed through the pericardium and the heart.[3]

Hermann Moedder, a German radiologist, simulated certain aspects of crucifixion with volunteer university students. He suspended students by their arms from overhead beams and measured the initial effects of crucifixion on the human body. He also researched the medical explanation for the side wound and came to the conclusion that the spear pierced both the pleural cavity and the heart. Moedder thought this could account for the flow of water and blood which is both reported in the gospels and clearly seen on the Shroud.[4]

Another medical researcher was Giovanni Judica-Cordiglia, professor of forensic medicine at the University of Milan, and a scientific member of the 1969 commission which studied the Shroud. He examined the bloodstains and the question of how they were transferred to the cloth.[5]

In the 1960s, English physician David Willis tabulated and evaluated previous medical studies on the Shroud. Willis did a prolonged study of the wounds, and concluded that the Shroud was authentic from the medical viewpoint. He agreed with Barbet, Moedder, and others that the lance pierced the heart.[6]

American physician Anthony Sava studied the wounds on the Shroud over several decades, paying special attention to the possibility that scourging caused internal hemorrhaging in Jesus' chest.[7]

The forensic specialist on the Shroud of Turin Research Project team is pathologist Robert Bucklin, deputy medical examiner for Los Angeles County. Bucklin, the leading pathologist in the post-1978 Shroud research, has been chiefly concerned with the nature of the wounds of the man buried in the Shroud. Along with other medical examiners, he believes that the chest wound was caused by a lance that pierced both the pleural cavity and the heart.[8]

All of these many medical experts, physicians, and anatomists are convinced of a major fact—that the man in the Shroud was definitely dead. As Ricci notes, it is evident that we are dealing with a real corpse who has suffered real wounds from crucifixion.[9] As we have seen, it is probably Jesus who is dead and buried.

Two facts about the Shroud image reveal that Jesus was dead. First, his body is in a state of rigor mortis. Bucklin notes that the body is very definitely stiff and rigid. Also, the left leg has been drawn back up into the position it occupied during crucifixion, being affixed there by rigor mortis.[10] Another example is that Jesus' head is definitely bent forward in a position fixed by rigor mortis. The three-dimensional image analysis of the cloth has verified this forward bending of the body at the point of death. Jesus was leaning out from the cross; after death, his body was frozen in this position.[11] The Gospel of John also records that Jesus bowed his head forward at death (19:30).

Second, we know Jesus was dead because the blood flow on the Shroud from the chest wound took place after death. For instance, the head wounds are pre-mortem while the chest wound is post-mortem. The post-mortem nature of the chest wound is detectable by the fact that the blood did not spurt outwards from this wound. Rather, the blood from the chest cavity oozed out slowly without any pressure from a beating heart, like blood oozing out from a punctured bag.[12]

The Doubts About Jesus' Death

A surprising number of people believe or suspect that Jesus did not really die on the cross, but somehow escaped death, revived in the tomb, and rejoined his disciples. The disciples regarded his reappearance as miraculous—a resurrection. This view is sometimes popularly held among Muslims and other non-Christians. Many people who are unwilling to face the Bible's call to faith explain the resurrection of Jesus in these terms.

This "swoon theory" even had a short life among critical biblical scholars in the nineteenth century. David Strauss, a liberal critic himself, dispensed with the swoon theory with some simple reasoning and pointed questions.[13]

Even if it was imagined that Jesus survived the rigors of crucifixion, what about the stone in the entrance of the tomb? In his severely weakened condition, could Jesus move this object up the trough in front of the opening? This would require great strength even for a healthy man, especially when it is considered that the flat surface of the stone *inside* the tomb would allow no outcropping against which one's weight might be used.

But even if he was able to get out of the tomb, what about his ability to walk the distance to where his disciples were, on feet that had held his weight suspended on a Roman spike just a few days previous?

However, the most convincing refutation of the theory concerns Jesus' arrival at the location where his disciples were staying. Whatever else is supposed, it is not doubted that Jesus would have been in extremely serious physical condition, bleeding, pale, limping and in need of help. He would not have looked like the resurrected Lord of Life! As Strauss pointed out, the disciples would have gotten a doctor rather than proclaiming Jesus risen! Yet the disciples did proclaim him the resurrected, glorified Lord of Life.

At the turn of the century, Albert Schweitzer proclaimed Strauss' critiques convincing.[14] This hypothesis not only lost supporters, but other critical observers in the early years of the twentieth century proclaimed that the swoon theory was only a curious view of the past. It was no longer considered a viable alternative even for critical scholars.[15]

Modern data has added more criticisms against the swoon theory. Two considerations should be briefly mentioned. First, as we described above, crucifixion involves asphyxiation. Hanging in the "down position" induces death and no amount of feigning is going to allow the body to get air which is not available to the lungs. The Romans were quite aware of this, as indicated by the skeleton of Yohanan, the crucifixion victim mentioned earlier. His broken ankles not only provide archaeological confirmation of the gospel accounts of crucifixion, but point directly to the Roman's knowledge that the end result of crucifixion is death by asphyxiation. Jesus' ankles were not broken because the Romans were fully convinced that he was already dead. If he had not died, it may be said that this method would have sealed his fate as well. Either way, the end result of death is very probable.

Second, and even more useful in refuting the swoon theory, is the medical conclusion that the Roman spear pierced Jesus' heart. Even apart from the Shroud research, a conclusion can be given. There is a strong indication that Jesus was already dead before he was stabbed, but even if he was still alive, medical scholars indicate that it would certainly have killed him. Thus, the chest wound would also disprove the thesis that Jesus did not die on the cross. Therefore, it is no surprise that the swoon theory is rejected today even by critical scholars.[16]

In addition to all of this data, the Shroud provides a final twofold death blow to the swoon theory. As pointed out earlier, this cloth provides two empirical considerations which reveal that Jesus did die on the cross. First, the body is in a state of rigor mortis, indicating his death due to crucifixion. Second, the post-mortem nature of the chest wound is clearly revealed, which is a further indication of Jesus' death. Combined, we have solid scientific evidence of Jesus' death, which entirely abrogates the swoon theory. Thus we are left with the reality of Jesus' physical death due to Roman crucifixion.

Death By Crucifixion

The evidence of the Shroud shows that Jesus died by crucifixion. However, while the exact cause of death is rather difficult to determine, medical scholars can get very close to a specific answer. Crucifixion was a form of execution practiced by many ancient peoples, but not very frequently in the last two thousand years. Medical researchers have had to study crucifixion carefully in order to understand it.[17]

Many factors contribute to death by crucifixion. In the case of Jesus, he was tortured in other ways as well. He was severely scourged, crowned with thorns, beaten in the face, and forced to carry a heavy cross for at least a short distance. He was crucified by being nailed to a cross through both his wrists and feet. After his death, he was stabbed in the side of the chest with a Roman lance. It is difficult to isolate a single cause of death among these brutal tortures.

Most researchers agree that death by crucifixion is essentially a slow death by asphyxiation. Crucifixion kills by forcing a victim to take a certain position on a cross. The weight of the body causes the pectoral muscles in the chest to constrict, causing much pain. Eventually, the pectoral and intercostal muscles become paralyzed so that they cannot force air out of the lungs. The victim can inhale, but not exhale. Thus, as long as the body hangs in the "down" position on the cross, asphyxiation begins. Death follows if the position is not changed.

The victim breathes by pushing up on the nails in his feet a few inches to relieve pressure on the chest muscles. This allows him to exhale, but this maneuver causes excruciating pain in the ankles. Therefore, the victim slumps back down into the previous position and asphyxiation begins again. This up-and-down process is repeated as long as the victim has the strength, or until his executioners break his ankles. Sometimes death did not come for days. Jesus probably uttered his statements from the cross during the times when he pushed up.

Hermann Moedder, the German radiologist, performed an experiment with volunteer university students in order to ascertain how long it took a crucifixion victim to lose consciousness while suspended in the "down" position. He tied the volunteers to a crossbeam, and found that they began to lapse into unconsciousness in a maximum of twelve minutes. Others have performed similar experiments in which the person remained conscious somewhat longer than this.[18] The difference in time of consciousness was caused by variations in strength, weight, and physical stamina of the volunteer, as well as in the exact experimental method used. Yet the conclusion was clear: unless the victim could push up to breathe, death came swiftly on the cross.

Thus, the significance of the practice of breaking a victim's legs becomes apparent. With broken legs, the victim could not push his body into the "up" position in order to breathe. The knotted and cramped arm muscles would no longer be able to pull the body up, and asphyxiation came quickly.[19]

The Shroud indicates that Jesus took this twofold position on the cross. Two blood flows, approximately ten degrees apart, can be readily perceived on the forearms, especially on the left arm. This indicates that Jesus took two positions on the cross, each with the arm turned at a different angle. He did this in order to breathe, and to relieve some of the pain caused by remaining in the "down" position too long.[20]

The Side Wound

One of the most intriguing aspects of the Shroud image is the graphic evidence of the spear wound in Jesus' chest. The Gospel of John states that he was already dead when he was stabbed in the side in order to make sure that he was dead, and that blood and water proceeded from the wound. This mixture is visible on the Shroud. It proceeded from the chest wound, and is actually more visible on the dorsal image, where the blood flowed horizontally across the waist. Physicians agree that the Shroud image of the wound is consistent with the gospel statement that a Roman lance penetrated Jesus' heart. However, the experts have similar but somewhat differing explanations for the presence of the water as well as blood in the flow from the wound.[21]

One view concerns the pericardium, the sac which surrounds the heart, and which contains a small amount of watery fluid. When the body undergoes great stress, as crucifixion would certainly entail, the amount of fluid increases and the sac expands. The Roman lance would then have passed through Jesus' pericardium and into the right side of his heart, which is filled with blood even after death. As the lance was withdrawn, it would draw out the blood from the heart and the watery fluid from the expanded pericardium.[22]

Anthony Sava, an American physician, has a different explanation for the water flow. He believes that the severe scourging caused internal hemorrhaging in Jesus' chest, and the pleural cavity filled with blood. The blood settled on the bottom of the chest cavity while a clear liquid was left on top. Sava says that the Roman lance entered the chest and, upon being withdrawn, released the blood and the water from the chest.[23]

Both of these views may be partially correct. The lance could have passed through the pleural cavity, through the pericardium and into the heart. The blood could have come both from the pleural cavity and from the right side of the heart, while the water could have come from both the upper chest cavity and from the pericardium. Indeed, this combination is the general view held by the German radiologist Moedder and by English physician David Willis.[24]

The most probable thesis is that held by Bucklin, who agrees with Moedder and Willis that the lance pierced both the pleural cavity and the right side of the heart. He opposes Sava's theory that there was severe hemorrhaging in the chest, since the chest injuries were not severe enough. However, Bucklin agrees that most of the water proceeded from pleural effusion while most of the blood came from the right side of the heart.[25]

The explanations for the blood and water flow are closely related at several points. All physicians who have examined the question agree that Jesus was already dead when the chest wound was inflicted. The blood and water most probably flowed from both the heart and the chest cavity.

The Physical Cause of Jesus' Death

Physicians who have examined the Shroud image are unanimous in their belief that the man was dead when he was placed in the Shroud, and that his death was caused by crucifixion and the tortures that preceeded it. They also agree that he was dead when the spear pierced his side. They are not as sure about the *exact* cause of Jesus' death, but their opinions are quite similar.

Most experts hold that Jesus died primarily of asphyxiation, the usual cause of death in crucifixion. According to this view, Jesus died more quickly than most crucifixion victims because scourging and beating had gravely weakened him. He was eventually unable to pull himself up on the cross in order to breathe, and he asphyxiated in the "down" position on the cross. In this case, the muscles around his lungs kept him from exhaling and directly caused his death. Bucklin adds that complications due to congestive heart failure were likely as well.[26]

Sava offers a related alternative. He holds that the internal hemorrhaging in the chest cavity caused by the fierce scourging was a cause of death. These liquids slowly compressed the lungs, causing asphyxiation by pleural effusion.[27]

Davis presents another somewhat similar view. He holds that the pericardium, the sac surrounding the heart, filled with fluid under the stress of suffering. This liquid compressed the heart, eventually causing heart failure. After Jesus was dead, the Roman lance pierced both the pericardium and the heart, and released the blood and watery fluid.[28]

A consensus is visible among these views. Most scholars hold that asphyxiation played an important part in Jesus' death. He struggled on the cross to keep breathing. Some scholars hold that he asphyxiated directly when the chest muscles failed to sustain breathing. Others suggest asphyxiation as the blood and fluid also compressed his lungs. But all these scholars agree that the Shroud contains conclusive evidence that Jesus indeed died and that it reveals the general features of his death.

We should not let this examination of the physical causes for Jesus' death distract us from the fact that he gave up his life freely according to the witness of the gospels.[29] The New Testament also says that Jesus died for a specific purpose—as a sacrifice for the sins of mankind (John 3:16). This is the claim both of Jesus[30] and of the New Testament as a whole.[31] The Shroud directly reveals nothing concerning these specific claims, but we will ascertain in Chapter Twelve if there are other reasons to accept their validity.

ELEVEN

Evidence for the Resurrection?

WE NOW COME TO a pivotal point in our investigation of the Shroud of Turin. It is very important to know that the Shroud is a genuine artifact and that it is very probably the burial garment of Jesus. We can also learn much from this linen cloth about the physical cause of Jesus' death. However, the most crucial issue is whether the Shroud offers scientific evidence for Jesus' resurrection. The scientific investigation reveals some extremely interesting facts on this subject, especially when seen in the context of historical evidence. We will examine this scientific and historical evidence in this chapter.

The Cause of the Image

One of the most interesting of these scientific facts is the mystery of the process that formed the image on the cloth. This is one of the most intriguing aspects of the Shroud, one with great possible relevance to the truth of the gospel's witness

that Jesus died, and rose again. At the risk of repeating ourselves, let us review what we know about this image formation
process.

The hypotheses for the cause of the image divide into three
general categories. Fraud hypotheses suggest that paints, dyes,
powder, or acid were applied to the linen by brush, another
kind of applicator, or by direct contact. The second set of
hypotheses suggest that a natural process formed the image on
the shroud, by means of a vaporgraph or direct contact with
the dead body. The third category is the view that the image
was caused by some sort of light or heat.

As we have seen, there are many decisive reasons why the
fraud hypotheses have failed.[1] There is no foreign substance on
the Shroud that would account for the image.[2] There is no sign
of brush strokes or other type of application. In addition,
painting cannot account for the observed properties of the
image. Thus, there is a high probability that the Shroud is
authentic. Heller estimates the chances of the Shroud being
fraudulent as 1 in 10 million.[3]

Likewise, neither can natural processes such as direct contact
or vaporgraph adequately account for the formation of the
image. Both fraud and natural hypotheses fail to account for
such phenomena as the three-dimensional, superficial and non-
directional qualities of the image, and the fact that there are no
plateaus or saturation points on the image fibers. Such hypotheses are also opposed by the image density, lack of distortion,
the shading, and color distribution. The fire and water damage
of 1532 did not alter the chemical structure of the image, as it
would have if the image was a painting. The image was not
caused by vapor diffusion, because vapor does not travel in
either straight or parallel lines. In other words, scientific studies reveal that the Shroud image cannot have been created by
direct contact, fraud, or vapors.[4]

What about the image being caused by light or heat? Before
the 1978 investigation, some scientists thought this theory was
the most probable, and it now remains the most probable not
only because the alternative views seem to be eliminated, but

also by several highly sophisticated scientific tests of the light-heat hypothesis.

John Heller and Alan Adler, chemists who were especially concerned with determining the physical and chemical characteristics of the Shroud image, have reinforced the fact that the image was caused by the oxidation, dehydration, and conjugation of the fibrils. In the laboratory, Heller and Adler reversed this oxidation and dehydration process present in the Shroud image in order to get back to the cause of these processes. Then they checked their experimental results both physically and chemically and confirmed their earlier results, which had ascertained that the chemical changes on the image fibrils reacted as if they were caused by heat.[5]

There are other indications that the Shroud image was caused by heat or light. In particular, the spectrophotometric data gathered by Gilbert and Gilbert have provided very strong supporting evidence for such scorch hypotheses. These sensitive experiments examined the molecular properties of the Shroud image, and determined that the image color is almost identical to the spectrum of the 1532 fire of the same optical density.[6] In other words, the properties of the image are nearly identical to the properties of the burn marks sustained from the fire. This indicates that the cause of the burn (heat, light) is probably similar to the cause of the image. These tests strongly indicate that the source of the image was a light or heat scorch. (See Appendix B.)

In addition, the Shroud image has several properties which resemble properties of a scorch. The superficiality of the image, the absence of any plateaus or saturation, the image's stability in heat and water, and its coloration are not only very difficult to explain by alternative theses, but are actually properties of a scorch. A scorch also causes the oxidation, dehydration, and conjugation of the fibrils observed on the Shroud. These are likewise reactions which are produced by scorching. Again the scorch conclusion is indicated by the facts.

The evidence here is such that Rogers and Jumper asserted that the Shroud image "is so similar in integrated response to that of the scorch that the inference that the 'body' image is chemically similar to a scorch is inescapable."[7]

The highly sensitive tests mentioned earlier (such as those of Heller and Adler and Gilbert and Gilbert) are able to measure physical and chemical properties to a very fine degree. Thus they are excellent indicators of the composition of the image. The fact that these tests agree that the image is very similar to a scorch is truly an important indication of the image's molecular nature. This fact also increases the probability of a heat or light scorch conclusion.

Therefore, we reach the conclusion that the image on the Shroud was probably caused by a heat or light scorch. This is the most probable thesis as indicated by three lines of argumentation. First, there is an absence of viable alternative hypotheses. Second, there is much evidence in favor of a scorch, evidence provided by several sensitive scientific tests. Third, the physical and chemical properties of the Shroud image are characteristics of a scorch. In particular, the tests of the physical and chemical composition of the image by Heller and Adler provide strong confirming verification of our conclusion that the image was caused by a heat or light scorch.

The next question is obvious: what caused this scorch? That a dead body could produce heat and light is surely intriguing, especially in light of the failure of alternative hypotheses to explain the image. Yet such a heat or light scorch is the probable result supported by the scientific evidence.

Before we discuss the probable cause of the scorch in more detail, we should examine the evidence for the resurrection of Jesus Christ. What does history tell us of this event?

The Historicity of Jesus' Resurrection

The Shroud's contribution to an understanding of Jesus' resurrection is the most recent development in a debate which has been raging intensely for more than two hundred years. This is the battle between skeptics who doubt the historical character of Jesus' resurrection and those who defend it. Indeed, the argument dates back to the beginning of the church, and the skeptical attack on the resurrection continues to this day. We will now present a historical defense of the resurrection in as much detail as this chapter allows. What does history say about the resurrection? How do skeptics challenge it?

The testimony of the disciples was the basis for the proclamation of faith in the early church. The gospels relate this faith that death was not the end for Jesus, but that he was raised from the dead by God. History provides strong verification for this belief.

We cannot state the historical arguments for Jesus' resurrection in detail here. However, we will provide a brief summary of a detailed historical apologetic for the resurrection which this author (Habermas) has defended in depth elsewhere.[8]

Our argument for the historicity of the resurrection rests on three major points: (1) no one has advanced a plausible naturalistic explanation for the resurrection of Jesus which accounts for the known historical facts about it; (2) the literal resurrection of Jesus is corroborated by a number of established historical facts; and (3) a few known and virtually undisputed historical facts alone are sufficient to build a probable case for this event.

Naturalistic Explanations. It is no wonder that critics have long challenged the fact of Jesus' resurrection from the dead. The resurrection is the very center of the Christian faith (1 Corinthians 15:12-20). Jesus' resurrection is the basis for the Christian claims that he lives today and that eternal life is also offered to men who turn to him. The implications of his conquest of death are inescapable.

Critics and skeptics have proposed various natural explanations for the resurrection. These theories attempt to explain this event in terms of the normal operations of nature. Most of these naturalistic theories became popular in the nineteenth century when the intellectual climate of the time was hostile to the miraculous. Some of them date back to the time of Christ, when civil and religious authorities in Jerusalem were confronted with the problem of explaining the empty tomb. The "swoon theory," refuted in the last chapter, is a typical naturalistic theory of the resurrection. This theory explains the resurrection by simply denying that Jesus died. We will deal with other specific naturalistic theories in more detail later in the chapter.

These naturalistic theories have failed for at least five reasons. The initial point is that each of the alternative theories falls prey to a number of criticisms. In other words, theories which rely on naturalistic proposals have been refuted by several key objections which render each one quite improbable.[9]

Second, combinations of such theories do not account for the known historical facts surrounding the resurrection any better than individual theories do. Each individual theory leaves major facts unexplained, and no combination of naturalistic solutions is found to be viable. Each theory has individually been shown to be improbable; combinations only compound the improbability.

The third reason for rejecting naturalistic theories concerns David Hume's essay "Of Miracles." Hume's rejection of the miraculous has had great influence, yet his work exhibits numerous flaws and fails noticeably in its attempt to reject miracles,[10] as even critics admit.[11] Miraculous events cannot be ruled out for the reasons Hume states. Those who have been influenced by Hume and use his general methodology are also incorrect. We will critique these arguments in more detail in the next chapter.

Fourth, we are also justified in rejecting naturalistic theories because nineteenth-century liberal scholars themselves rejected them. Even those who followed Hume in dismissing miracles could not agree on a convincing explanation for the resurrection—the greatest of miracles. They succeeded in refuting each other's hypotheses, thus leaving no viable alternative.[12]

Fifth, most twentieth-century critical scholars have dismissed naturalistic theories of the resurrection. While liberal scholars in the nineteenth century critiqued each other's views individually, critics in the twentieth century have rejected them as a whole, judging that they are incapable of explaining the known data. For instance, Raymond Brown, the Catholic scripture scholar, asserts that naturalistic theories are no longer even respectable among twentieth-century critical scholars. They have rejected these alternative views and any popularized renditions of them.[13] Such rejections are frequent in the works of recent critics.

However, the attack on the resurrection has been revised and modernized in the twentieth century. Critical scholars who are skeptical about Jesus' resurrection seldom propose classic naturalistic theories to explain the gospel accounts. Instead, they "reinterpret" the scripture and propose a "spiritual" resurrection. The important thing, they say, is not that Jesus literally rose from the dead, but that the disciples were convinced he did. Jesus was "alive" in the minds of his followers, and he "lives" today in those who believe in him as he existentially confronts men today. Some critics additionally assert that "something happened," but we do not know what it was.

Such a critical "reinterpretation" of the resurrection is entirely incompatible with biblical Christianity. As St. Paul put it, "if Christ was not raised, your faith is worthless. . . . If our hopes in Christ are limited to this life only, we are the most pitiable of men" (1 Corinthians 15:17-19). These contemporary attempts to deny the historicity of the literal resurrection of Christ are also vulnerable to at least three critiques. We will briefly mention them here.

First, to hold that Jesus did not literally rise from the dead implies that a natural explanation exists for the events related in the gospels. Yet, as just shown, there are no viable alternative hypotheses which can explain the known historical facts. Even critical scholars admit this. This is a serious limitation to hypotheses of a "spiritual" resurrection.

Second, the positive historical case for Jesus' resurrection is very strong. As will be shown below, the minimum number of known historical facts, ones which are accepted even by critical scholars, provide a strong basis to show the probability of Jesus' literal resurrection. This disproves these contemporary views on historical grounds. In short, there is no good reason to seriously entertain contemporary reinterpretations when the critically established historical facts alone are sufficient to make a probable case for Jesus' literal resurrection.

Third, adherents of the "spiritual reinterpretation" are being illogical if, as they often do, they continue to claim some unique significance for Jesus' resurrection. Their "spiritual" Jesus would be no more alive today than any other dead person of history whose memory is still cherished by living men and women. If Jesus did not literally rise from the dead, there is questionable linguistic value to the word "risen."

Thus we have seen that naturalistic theories are weak. Each theory is beset by many objections which invalidate it as a viable hypothesis, and combinations of such improbable theories also fail to account for the known facts. In addition, Hume's attack on miracles is invalid, thus eliminating it and similar reasoning as the traditional backdrop for rejecting miraculous events. Nineteenth-century liberal scholars destroyed each alternative theory individually, while twentieth-century critical scholars of various schools of thought have rejected these theories wholesale. Thus naturalistic alternative hypotheses have thereby been shown to be unable to account for the facts concerning Jesus' resurrection.

Historical Evidence for the Resurrection. The second defense of the resurrection is the strength of the historical case for it. Historians and even critical scholars who study the gospels accept a number of reliable historical facts surrounding the resurrection. They have done so even by viewing the gospels as normal, ancient documents.

Virtually all scholars today agree that Jesus was a historical figure who died by crucifixion and that his body was afterwards buried. His death made his disciples despondent; they believed all hope was gone.

According to many contemporary scholars, Jesus' tomb was found empty a few days later, but this in itself did not cause belief in the disciples. However, virtually all scholars agree that soon afterwards the disciples had experiences which they were convinced were appearances of the risen Jesus. Their lives were transformed as they believed that Jesus was indeed alive. These experiences emboldened them to preach and witness in Jerusalem, the very place where Jesus had been crucified and buried only a short time before, a city full of his enemies. The core of their message, the central proclamation of these eyewitnesses, was that Jesus had risen from the dead.

History also relates that the Christian church was born and grew because of this testimony and that Sunday was the primary day of worship for the new church. Most scholars add that James, one of the early church leaders, was a skeptic who was converted when he was convinced that he also saw the risen Jesus. All agree that Paul of Tarsus, a persecutor of the church, was converted to Christianity by an experience which he also believed was an appearance of the risen Jesus.

These are the minimum number of historical facts agreed on by almost all scholars, whatever their school of thought. They consider these facts to be knowable history. Any alternate explanation—naturalistic or modernist "reinterpretation"—must be able to account for these facts. These are the facts that constitute the second major contemporary defense of the resurrection.

We will consider these facts in more detail. From this summary, we will focus on nine historical facts which support the historical and literal nature of the resurrection. A tenth argument will also be added. Since these facts are established by historical procedures, their historical basis is admitted by virtually all scholars.

Perhaps the strongest historical argument for Jesus' resurrection is the disciples' eyewitness experiences of what they believed to be literal appearances of the risen Jesus. This is a key argument both because there are no viable naturalistic hypotheses which can account for these experiences and because there are other indications that the eyewitness testimony is accurate, as we will see.

Second, the disciples were transformed from fearful men who were afraid to be identified with Jesus into bold witnesses who proclaimed faith in Christ in the midst of his enemies. They were even willing to die for their faith, a strong indication that they really saw the risen Jesus. Indeed, the disciples claimed that they believed precisely because they had been eyewitnesses of his resurrection appearances.

A third fact is the empty tomb. Many scholars admit that Jesus' tomb really was empty on Sunday morning, as even early extra-biblical historical sources attest.

A fourth historical argument for the resurrection is the fact that Jesus' resurrection was the very center of early Christian preaching by the original eyewitnesses. Even historical-critical studies conclude that the teaching about the resurrection dates virtually from the time of the eyewitness experiences themselves. Thus, it was not a later legend added to the Christian message.[14]

Fifth, the Jewish leaders could not disprove the disciples' claim that Jesus had risen, even though they had both a motive and the power to do so.[15] These leaders were located in the very city in which the disciples claimed that Jesus rose. They had the means to check these claims and examine the empty tomb. Yet, these enemies of Christ could not disprove the message. Their failure to do so supports the truthfulness of the disciples' message.

The sixth fact is that the Christian church promptly began, grew, and flourished, with the center of its worship and evangelism being the proclamation of Jesus' resurrection. The phenomenon of the church is another indication of the original event.

Seventh, Sunday became the day of Christian worship (Acts 20:7; 1 Corinthians 16:2). This is unusual because the earliest Christians were monotheistic Jews who were taught to worship on Saturday. The best explanation is that Sunday was the day of Christ's resurrection; otherwise there is no adequate reason why this day was chosen for worship.

The eighth and ninth facts are that two nonbelieving skeptics, James and Paul, both became zealous Christians after having experiences which they also believed to be appearances of the risen Jesus. Even a critical scholar such as Reginald Fuller concludes that even if the appearance to James was not recorded by Paul (1 Corinthians 15:7), such an occurrance would still have to be postulated anyway in order to account for both James' conversion and his subsequent promotion to a position of high authority in the early church.[16] Paul's dramatic conversion is an even more convincing piece of evidence, since this new believer had been a famous persecutor of Christians. Paul's experience alone complicates any attempt to formulate a naturalistic explanation for the resurrection.[17]

Our tenth fact, not covered in the historical summary, is that Jesus predicted his resurrection ahead of time. Although these predictions are not usually admitted by critical scholars, they are supported by several historical considerations. These predictions thereby reveal that the resurrection was a planned occurrence performed by God. We will return to a further treatment of this point in Chapter Twelve.

When combined with the failure of the naturalistic theories, this minimum of ten historical facts provides a strong case for the historicity of Jesus' resurrection. This case is especially strong because these facts are based on recognized history.[18] Particularly persuasive are the eyewitness experiences of the disciples, James, and Paul, along with their corresponding personal transformations. In short, the historical resurrection of Jesus is the best explanation for the known facts, especially since the naturalistic theories have failed. Critical historian William Wand sums up the conclusion about the resurrection very well:

All the strictly historical evidence we have is in favor of it, and those scholars who reject it ought to recognize that they do so on some other ground than that of scientific history.[19]

Therefore, it may be concluded that the resurrection is a probable historical event. An additional apologetic will strengthen this case even further.

The "Core" Historical Facts. Earlier, a number of facts were enumerated as knowable history, accepted as such by virtually all scholars. We can further establish the historicity of the resurrection by using only four of these historical facts which are accepted as factual even by critics. These four facts are: (1) Jesus' death due to crucifixion; (2) the disciples' subsequent eyewitness experiences which they were convinced were literal appearances of the risen Jesus; (3) the corresponding transformation of the disciples; and (4) Paul's conversion experience, which he also believed was an appearance of the risen Jesus.

These four facts provide a mini-apologetic for Jesus' literal resurrection, as they are able, for instance, to both disprove the naturalistic theories and to provide some major positive evidences which establish the historicity of this event.[20] A few examples will now point out these claims.

First, these four "core" historical facts alone disprove naturalistic theories of the resurrection. For instance, the swoon theory is ruled out both by the fact of Jesus' death (see Chapter Ten) and by Paul's conversion. The disciples' experiences disprove the hallucination and other subjective theories both because such phenomena are not collective or contagious, being observed by one person alone, and because of the wide variety of time and place factors involved. Paul, who was on his way to persecute Christians, certainly was not in the proper psychological frame of mind to have a hallucination. The fact that it was the disciples and other earliest eyewitnesses who had these actual experiences likewise rules out the argument that the resurrection is a legend or myth, since the *original* teaching concerning the resurrection is therefore based on real eyewitness testimony. It was not a later legend (as the creed in 1 Cor 15:3ff emphatically reveals). Likewise, Paul was obviously not converted from skepticism by a legend. Lastly, the stolen body and other fraud theories are disproven by the disciples' transformation. Their change shows that they really believed that Jesus rose from the dead, as critics admit. Additionally liars would not have become martyrs. Similarly, Paul would not have been convinced by any fraud.[21]

Second, these four "core" facts in themselves provide the major positive evidence for Jesus' literal resurrection from the dead.[22] Jesus died; his disciples were convinced they saw him risen again; the disciples' experiences have not been explained away naturalistically; they were transformed into men willing to die for their faith; and Paul, an intelligent, committed enemy of Christ, later also had such an experience and was transformed. When this evidence is considered together, the historical resurrection is shown to be the best explanation for the facts, especially since the facts have not been accounted for in any other way.

Furthermore, since these "core" facts (and the earlier accepted facts in general) have been *established by historical-critical procedures*, contemporary scholars cannot then reject this evidence simply by referring to "discrepancies" in the New Testament texts or to its general "unreliability." Not only are such critical claims refuted by much evidence, most of which is not discussed here, but the literal resurrection can be historically demonstrated even by the minimum number of historical facts. Neither can it be said only that "something" happened, the nature of which we cannot know because of naturalistic premises, the character of history, or the "cloudiness" or "legendary character" of the New Testament texts. Neither can it be said that Jesus rose spiritually, but not literally again, these and other such views are refuted by the facts admitted by virtually all scholars to be knowable history. They are adequate to historically demonstrate the literal resurrection of Jesus according to probability. While critical doubts may be present with regard to other issues, these accepted facts are sufficient in themselves to show the historical probability that Jesus rose from the dead.[23]

The Shroud and the Resurrection

What can the Shroud of Turin add to this historical verification for the literal resurrection of Jesus? The Shroud presents at least four further reasons for the probability of this event. In fact, the Shroud's evidence for the resurrection is so strong that if it is not Jesus' actual burial garment, then Christians might have to consider the possibility that someone else rose from the dead!

First, Jesus' body did not decompose while wrapped in the Shroud. Jesus' body is in a state of rigor mortis, and pathologists are sure he was dead. But, beyond these initial signs of death, the scientific tests found no evidence for decomposition. The implication of this is clear. The absence of bodily decomposition on the Shroud reveals that Jesus' body was not in contact with the cloth for any prolonged period of time.

In a Middle Eastern environment in Jesus' time, severe bodily decomposition would occur even within four days. While experimental studies cannot assign any exact time period to Jesus' contact with the cloth, we can ascertain that his body did not remain in the Shroud long enough to cause any such advanced or severe decomposition. That is, his body was separated from the material after a comparatively short period of time.[24]

The second sign of the resurrection on the Shroud concerns the body's removal from the cloth. The facts militate against the body being removed from the Shroud by any human means because the bloodstains are intact. As we saw earlier, each bloodstain is characterized by anatomical correctness, including precisely outlined borders, with blood clots intact. If the cloth had been removed from the body, the blood clots would have smeared or broken. This precludes any separation of the body from the cloth by normal means.

A moment's reflection will reveal some of the medical reasoning here. When the linen was wrapped lengthwise around Jesus' body, it contacted the shed blood flowing from the head, the open chest wound, and the left wrist, feet, and elsewhere. As the blood dried, the linen would have become loosely attached to the wounds. Removing the Shroud, however carefully, would require both the removal of blood clots and the disturbing of the edges of the bloodstains. Since this did not happen with the Shroud, we may assert the probability that the body left the cloth in some way other than normal unwrapping of the Shroud. The contact bloodstains indicate that the body was not moved, rewrapped, or unwrapped.[25]

Third, it has already been noted that the image on the Shroud was probably caused by a heat or light scorch. Both because of the improbability of alternative natural hypotheses and because of the very nature of the image, we are confronted here with the problem of an extraordinary occurrence which has not been explained by natural means. As John Heller pointed out, speaking *scientifically*, the image "is a mystery."[26] The Shroud cannot provide proof for Jesus' resurrection. However, that Jesus' dead body probably produced a heat or light scorch, especially in view of the strong historical evidence for his resurrection, provides further corresponding probability for the fact that Jesus was raised from the dead. As Robert Bucklin points out, the Shroud provides supporting evidence for Jesus' resurrection.[27]

The fourth sign of the resurrection is the close correspondence among the Shroud, the gospels, and history. Because the Shroud is consistent with the gospel accounts at all other points, we have a strong argument that the Shroud corresponds to the gospel accounts of the resurrection as well. We found that the Shroud is probably an authentic archaeological artifact and the actual burial garment of Jesus. It is exactly consistent with the gospel accounts of the crucifixion procedure. Since the Shroud is probably Jesus', and since it corresponds so minutely to his death, why should it not also correspond to his resurrection, especially since the historical evidence indicates that he was raised from the dead? Once again, the historical facts lend even more credibility to the correspondence between the gospels and the Shroud concerning Jesus' resurrection.

Therefore, the Shroud provides at least four strong indications that Jesus probably did rise from the dead. The lack of real decomposition reveals that Jesus' body was not in contact with the Shroud for a prolonged period of time, meaning that his body was separated from the material after a comparatively short interrment. However, the intact bloodstains indicate that the body was probably not moved, rewrapped, or unwrapped. Then we find that Jesus' dead body most probably produced a heat or light scorch. These points, plus the close correspondence to the gospels and to history on these and related issues, all argue strongly for Jesus' resurrection. The total correspondence is simply amazing. Although proof is not available here, a very probable case for Jesus' resurrection has been provided. As Robert Bucklin asserts, "The medical data from the Shroud supports the resurrection. When this medical information is combined with the physical, chemical and historical facts, there is strong evidence for Jesus' resurrection."[28]

Evidence for the Resurrection

We have two very strong lines of evidence for the resurrection of Jesus. First, history provides a powerful apologetic for this event. The historical evidence indicates that Jesus rose in a changed or spiritual body, as perceived by the eyewitnesses. Building on the accepted historical facts, this conclusion is based on both the failure of the naturalistic theories and on the strong positive case for the literal appearances. When combined, these arguments show that Jesus' appearances are the best explanation for the facts. This argument is also supported by the known historical facts and especially by the "core" facts, which are sufficient to verify the probabilty of the resurrection. The critic's doubts on other issues thus do not change this basic conclusion. The literal resurrection of Jesus is a historical event. It is the best explanation of the historical evidence.

The other line of evidence for the resurrection comes from the scientific studies of the Shroud of Turin. These reveal that a dead body probably caused the image on the cloth by a light or heat scorch. The facts that there is no bodily decomposition (indicating bodily departure), that the bloodstains reveal that the body was not unwrapped, that dead bodies do not naturally cause such scorches, and that the Shroud of Jesus corresponds so closely to history and to the gospels are all very strong indications that the Shroud testifies to the resurrection of Jesus.

Many are hesitant to affirm Jesus' resurrection and will go to almost any extent in order to look for improbable alternative explanations for the historical facts and for the scientific Shroud data. But there is a point at which the skeptic must align himself with the facts and take an unbiased look at the evidence. Most scholars will agree that it is not acceptable to affirm a viewpoint just because it favors a miracle. But it is equally invalid to take any view, especially an improbable one, in order to avoid any chance of confronting a possible supernatural event.

When I (Habermas) was a factual agnostic with regards to

Jesus' resurrection, it was the historical evidence such as that outlined above that caused me to realize that Jesus probably did rise from the dead. But intellectual honesty causes me to say that if the same historical and scientific evidence existed for some other religious figure, I would be sufficiently challenged to investigate it. For instance, if the Shroud seemed to be that of Mohammed instead of Jesus, with all of the attending evidence, I would be bothered, but I would have to face the facts. However, there is no such evidence for Mohammed or any other person except Jesus. But then again, if I believed in naturalistic premises, I would be quite bothered by the historical and scientific evidence for Jesus' death and resurrection.

In conclusion, the historical arguments and the scientific arguments are very probable empirical indicators that Jesus did rise from the dead. When combined, they provide a strong twofold argument for this event. The converging evidence is not proof, but it does show that the literal, physical resurrection of Jesus of Nazareth is by far the best explanation for the physical, chemical, medical, and historical facts.

TWELVE

The Naturalism-Supernaturalism Debate: Do Miracles Occur?

THE INTELLECTUAL TEMPER OF our day is antagonistic to miracles. Modern scholars typically view nature as a uniform system of natural laws which behaves predictably and which, given time, man will understand completely. According to this naturalistic view, nature is sufficient to explain its own existence and all events which occur within it. On the other hand, the Christian has a supernatural point of view. The supernaturalist believes that God exists and may perform miracles on occasion for a specific purpose.

This naturalism-supernaturalism debate is an old one, and it still rages today. It is a philosophical debate with practical consequences. The naturalist point of view is the assumption behind secular humanism, a dominant value system in modern society. The secular humanist holds that man is the center of reality, and that God is irrelevant. The supernaturalist point of view, of course, is the assumption behind orthodox Christianity. The naturalism-supernaturalism conflict is an issue in many of the concerns that Christians have today.

This debate is relevant to the Shroud of Turin. The naturalism-supernaturalism question must be settled before we can end our discussion of the Shroud. In short, if God does not exist and if this is not a theistic universe, then an extraordinary act of God such as a miracle cannot occur. In other words, apart from a theistic context, the resurrection of Jesus would not be a miracle of God, but only a freak event of nature. Then someone with a naturalistic view would say that the Shroud is a strange, but natural, object which does not involve the action of God. However, if the resurrection occurred in a theistic context, then it would constitute evidence for a miracle. Thus the question of God's existence and action in miraculous events is crucial for our thesis.

A Brief Summary of the Debate

Prior to the seventeenth-century Enlightenment, few scholars rejected belief in miracles. However, doubts about miracles became widespread as the new rationalism spread in Europe. The Enlightenment intellectuals taught that the true authority for religion was reason, not the scriptures or church tradition. Thus, nothing in Christian belief could conflict with what reason said was true.

To the rationalist, the laws of nature were an insurmountable obstacle to miracles. Man's reason judged that miraculous events which would violate these laws would not occur. The rationalist will concede that there are strange events which may sometimes surpass human comprehension, but these events would always have natural explanations, and man should eventually discover these explanations. In short, the Enlightenment rationalists viewed miracles as needless intrusions into reality.

The Enlightenment efforts to dismiss the miraculous culminated in David Hume's essay "Of Miracles."[1] Hume defined a miracle as an event which violates the laws of nature through the volition of God or some other invisible agent. Hume's major thesis was that the laws of nature are uniform and thus do not allow for miracles. These laws are inalterable because the experience of mankind backs these laws. Hume thought this observation proved that miraculous events could not occur. In short, the laws of nature as supported by man's experience do not allow for miracles.[2]

Hume's effort became the pivotal argument among the many Enlightenment attempts to dismiss the miraculous. His essay was particularly influential among religious critics from the eighteenth century to the present who are skeptical and disbelieving about miraculous events.[3] David Strauss, a nineteenth-century liberal theologian, was quite representative of his fellow liberal scholars when he concluded that Hume's essay had shown that miracles could not occur, because events that violate the laws of nature do not happen.[4]

Hume's influence persists from his time to the present. Twentieth-century critical scholars have been strongly affected by Hume's argument against miracles.[5] Although contemporary scholars have updated his thesis, Hume's imprint is unmistakable.[6]

Many defenses of miracles have also appeared in response to these attacks. From the Enlightenment to the present, there have been numerous defenses of the philosophical, historical, and scientific bases for accepting these God-initiated events. In the twentieth century, the best-known of these contemporary defenses is probably C.S. Lewis' book *Miracles*, a refutation of Hume and other recent skeptics who attempt to dismiss the miraculous.[7]

Lewis and other orthodox Christians assert that the greatest of miracles is the resurrection of Jesus Christ. Skeptics and naturalists who follow the reasoning of Hume might hold that it is a freak natural event of nature. We will return below to both the major refutation of naturalistic views such as Hume's and a defense of God's action in miracles.

Two Contrasting World-Views

The naturalism-supernaturalism debate is joined at this point. A Christian apologist needs to ascertain if the literal resurrection of Jesus is indeed a miracle *performed by an act of God*. It is not enough to show, as we have done, that there is every reason to believe that this extraordinary event literally occurred in history—that Jesus Christ died, and was raised from death. To conclude that the resurrection happened is not the same as showing that it was performed by an act of God. For instance, theists might conclude that Jesus' resurrection is so extraordinary that only God could have caused it. However, naturalists might conclude that the resurrection is so strange that it must be a freak event of nature which we do not understand. In other words, the historicity of the resurrection alone does not completely answer the question of its cause. We must consider facts other than the historical data.

The underlying issue is a clash between two world-views. Do we live in a naturalistic or in a theistic universe? In a naturalistic universe, Jesus' resurrection would have to have some natural explanation; it would somehow be a product of the natural order. In a theistic universe, the resurrection would most likely be an orderly, planned occurrence brought about by God in order to fulfill a specific purpose. It would be a miracle performed by God.

Did God Perform the Resurrection?

For David Hume and other skeptics, miracles are virtually impossible because they violate the observed laws of nature, which are corroborated by man's experience of these laws. Even if God existed, he would not choose to reveal himself in a way that offends man's reason, meaning that he would not intervene in history with miraculous events.

Hume's thesis raises a number of interesting theological and logical issues. Since his skeptical views have exerted such influence on modern thought, we should examine them more closely.

Hume's position has numerous problems. Since they have been discussed in more detail elsewhere, we will focus only on the major critique here.[8] Hume postulates that the laws of nature are inviolate without ever ascertaining whether God exists and whether he has acted in history by temporarily suspending these laws. Hume therefore did not even ask the right question. He ruled out miracles from the start, by dismissing the possibility that we inhabit a theistic universe, presided over and ruled by a God who may not choose to be constrained by the patterns in nature which some call "laws." This possible activity of God is surely the major consideration in any discussion of miracles, yet Hume largely ignores God. He concentrates on the strength of nature's laws and mankind's experience of them without seriously asking whether a superior power superseded these laws. Thus his whole approach is badly flawed. In fact, it may be stated that *no amount* of arguing from naturalistic premises about the laws of nature can ever disprove the possibility that God exists, and that he has suspended nature's laws by performing a miracle in history by a power superior to those laws. If it could be shown that God probably performed a historical miracle, that would be good evidence, at that moment, for the existence of a power *superior* to the laws of nature.

Hume's critique has been updated and revised by others who have been skeptical about the miraculous, yet this fundamental critique applies to all of them. *No amount* of viewing the repeatable scientific evidence for nature's laws or for the strength of these laws can ever rule out the possibility that God intervened in history to perform a miracle by a *superior* power. It is fruitless to speak of the scientifically repeatable evidence for these laws if there is a stronger Power which could temporarily suspend them.

The issue we are considering thus boils down to the question of whether God exists and if he acts in history. God's action in miracles would indicate both that he does indeed exist and that his power is superior to nature's. In this issue, we are committed to finding the *best explanation* for the known facts.

To return to the question of this chapter: did God raise Jesus from the dead, or is the resurrection a freak event with an unknown but natural explanation? Is this a theistic universe, or one which can explain itself? There are at least two strong and independent lines of argumentation for asserting that God does exist, and that Jesus' resurrection was an extraordinary miracle performed by him, thereby validating a supernatural universe and refuting naturalistic premises.

The Prospective Argument

First, valid theistic arguments reveal that God does exist. Such arguments cannot be defended in the scope of this chapter. However, we will briefly describe two of these probable indicators of God's existence—the cosmological arguments from existential causality and the second law of thermodynamics.

Briefly, the cosmological argument from existential causality begins with the actual existence of finite human beings. By our very nature, we cannot explain or account for our own existence. Neither can our parents, or their parents. In fact, we cannot find an origin for this existence no matter how far we regress backwards, even in an infinite series of finite explanations for this present existence, for this does not make it any more possible to explain the origin of present existence. Thus there must be an infinite uncaused cause of current existence. This argument begins with actual existence, and requires an actual cause. It should not be confused with more familiar forms of the cosmological argument which rely on logical necessity. The existential argument requires us to postulate the actual existence of an infinite cause.[9]

The second law of thermodynamics states that the energy in the universe is moving irreversibly toward greater randomness or entropy. It is, in fact, running down to an eventual heat death. This indicates that the universe is not infinite, and the fact that it is running down reveals that it had a beginning at a point in time. The only ultimate beginning for a finite universe would be an infinite cause. At this point the second law actually becomes another cosmological argument for God's existence: the finite universe cannot explain its own existence. It had to originate from an infinite cause behind it.[10]

An even stronger case for God's existence may be made by combining a number of more-or-less traditional theistic arguments. The individual arguments are sufficient in themselves to show that God probably exists. Combined, they make the conclusion that he exists even stronger.

For instance, various other cosmological arguments may be used in conjunction with teleological and moral arguments to provide further converging reasons for concluding that God does exist. In short, the combination of these arguments reveals that God's existence is the best explanation for all of the facts.

It is interesting to note that scientific theories work much the same way. As Richard Swinburne points out, the Quantum Theory of the behavior of atomic particles does not rest on any one set of scientific observations, but rather on the convergence of data such as the photoelectric effect, the Compton effect, and the stability of atoms. By themselves they provide incomplete evidence for the Quantum Theory. Together, however, they make the theory highly probable, and indeed the Quantum Theory is accepted by almost all physicists as the best explanation for the behavior of atomic and subatomic particles.

Theism is shown to be true in a similar way. God's existence is the best explanation for the known cosmological, teleological, and moral data. Each points to such a Being and, together, they strongly favor his existence.[11]

However, the usage of these theistic arguments provides two additional considerations. First, there is the advantage of having both more decisive arguments such as the cosmological arguments from existential causality and the second law of thermodynamics plus the added strength of other converging theistic data. Thus we have both the individual arguments which point strongly to God's existence and the converging arguments which are much stronger when combined. In this latter instance, as with many scientific theories, it is the combination of relevant data which makes the overall thesis highly probable. Thus, both decisive, single arguments and other converging arguments reveal that the existence of God is highly probable.

Second, these theistic arguments reveal more about God than the fact that he exists. They tell us something about what he is like in that various of his attributes are revealed. The cosmological argument from existential causality reveals, for instance, that the God who accounts for existence must be infinite, uncaused, eternal, omnipotent, unchangeable, simple, and one. It also indicates that God is nonspatial, non-temporal, and pure actuality.[12] The second law of thermodynamics shows that God is transcendent, and has intelligence, wisdom, and limitless power. It even reveals that God has the components of personality: he has an aesthetic nature and he can perform supernatural acts such as creation.[13] Other converging theistic arguments also include characteristics such as his power, that he has created an aesthetically pleasing universe, and that he possesses a moral nature.[14]

Therefore, it may be asserted with good reason that it is indeed highly probable that this is a theistic universe. As such, we have an important indication of the identity of the power that caused Jesus' resurrection. The validity of theistic argumentation, including the many attributes of God, and the orderliness of the universe indicate that the literal resurrection was most probably also an orderly event brought about by God's power, in keeping with his attributes, in order to validate a theistic truth-claim. In other words, proceeding *prospectively* from valid theistic arguments, God's attributes, and the order and purpose in the universe, the historical resurrection of Jesus seems to be an orderly theistic event which verifies a theistic message. God raised Jesus from the dead in accordance with his known attributes. This evidence is much more in agreement with the theistic world-view outlined earlier than with the notion that the resurrection had some unknown natural cause.[15]

The Retrospective Argument

Our second major reason for concluding that God performed the resurrection reverses the direction of the first. The prospective argument argues for the likelihood of a divinely caused resurrection on the basis of what we know about the existence and attributes of God. The second argument proceeds *retrospectively*. It combines the historical resurrection with Jesus' theistic message in order to argue back to God's previous existence and actions in this event. Thus, Jesus' resurrection plus his theistic claims also reveal that this is a theistic universe. The retrospective argument is more detailed and, again, can only be presented briefly and in outline form. The evidence for this argument has been set forth in extended form in another work by this author, which will provide both the background and validation for these claims.[16]

First, Jesus claimed to be Deity. This is evident by his *self-designations*, such as the titles of Son of Man[17] and Son of God.[18] It is also revealed by his *actions*, such as his claims that he could forgive sin[19] and his fulfillment of Old Testament messianic prophecy.[20] Jesus also made various claims to *authority*. He asserted that salvation was found only in himself[21] and that his authority superseded that of the Jewish leaders.[22] Further claims of Deity are indicated by the *reactions* of others who knew him best. The Jewish leaders rejected Jesus at least partially because he claimed to be the Messiah of Israel.[23] The apostles and the earliest church leaders ascribed to him the titles of Messiah, Lord, Son of God, and even God.[24] His personal claims, in particular, are important indications of Jesus' belief in a theistic universe.

Next, Jesus also believed that he was God's chosen messenger sent to proclaim a special message.[25] He additionally believed that his miracles were signs of God's approval of his ministry.[26] Even critical methodology reveals that Jesus made such claims concerning his ministry, message, and miracles.[27] That such a unique messenger was also uniquely raised from the dead, especially considering Jesus' view of his miracles, is an important indicator that God did raise him.

Another special portion of Jesus' claims concerns his predictions of his own resurrection before it occurred, especially since these can be verified.[28] This strongly indicates that God raised him according to plan in an orderly manner and that Jesus had foreknowledge of it.

But are Jesus' claims true? Jesus' claims to be both Deity and God's chosen messenger, his views concerning his corroborating miracles, and his predicted resurrection all attest to his theistic world-view. His claims, then, indicate that his resurrection was an orderly and planned occurrence. As such, he would be in the best position to interpret this literal event. Jesus taught that the resurrection validated his message and his claims. Additionally, the only time that a resurrection is known to have occurred, it happened to the only person who made these extraordinary claims concerning both himself and God. It is thus highly probable that the combination of this most unique historical event with the unique message of Jesus verifies Jesus' theistic world-view.

In other words, if just anyone had been raised from the dead the cause might be hard to discern. But since it was Jesus who was raised, we must take very seriously his claims to be Deity and that he was a special messenger, as well as his belief that his miracles, and his coming resurrection, in particular, validated these claims. Since these unique claims were coupled with the unique resurrection event, we judge that, in all probability, Jesus' theistic world-view was validated.

The Relevance of the Shroud

The Shroud of Turin may have an important bearing on the naturalism-supernaturalism debate. It has been stated by some that the research on the Shroud may initiate a very intense discussion of the evidence for God's action in human history. This view asserts that the Shroud studies might mount a serious reassessment of the naturalism which has recently dominated Western thinking.

It does indeed seem that the Shroud challenges the naturalistic world-view. There is no complete scientific explanation for the Shroud. Scientists can tell us much about the cloth—but only up to a point. They can describe the characteristics of the image, but not how it got there. Furthermore, both history and the Shroud provide strong evidence for something even more mysterious—the resurrection of Jesus Christ. In an age when physicists puzzle over black holes and quarks, and when psychologists study the nature of the mind and life after death, the Shroud of Turin should at least be taken seriously.

At any rate, the Shroud should cause skeptics to examine the evidence for Jesus' resurrection. This evidence comes from two complementary directions: history and scientific investigation of the Shroud. Skeptics who have long denied the supernatural should at least consider such strong empirical data. The evidence is weighty. Scientists would have no trouble considering such evidence for a natural event. In fact, if such evidence existed for such a natural event, it would probably have been accepted long ago. Modern science has long been based on the principle of peer criticism and self-correction. The time has now come for such a reopening of the question of supernaturalism, even if it means that naturalism can no longer explain all of reality. Such a reassessment is demanded by the facts of both history and science.

Jesus' Call To Salvation

Since this is a theistic universe ruled by a God who sent his Son to proclaim a unique message, we should be impressed by the nature of Jesus' claims. As virtually all theologians agree, Jesus' central message concerned the Kingdom of God and the entrance requirements necessary for one to participate in the eternal blessings of the Kingdom. His chief theme was a call to personal decision with regards to one's eternal destiny.[29]

According to this central message, Jesus proclaimed that all men are sinners by nature and need forgiveness of their sins (Luke 24:47; Mark 8:38). The remedy is Jesus' substitutionary death and shed blood which pays for these sins (Mark 10:45; Matthew 26:28), an act which was completed by his resurrection from the dead (Luke 24:46-47; John 6:47). Faith in Jesus and his teachings and surrender to him allows one to gain entrance into the Kingdom of God and eternal life (Mark 1:15; John 3:15-16). Afterwards, our response should be total commitment to his claims (Luke 14:25-35).

Since this Kingdom message was Jesus' central theme, it was especially confirmed by his resurrection. In other words, we have concluded that his theistic message·was verified by his being raised from the dead. Therefore, this verification applies most of all to this specific portion of his theistic world-view in that God would have especially validated this theme in particular, as Jesus' central message.[30] Therefore, Jesus' call to salvation should not be disregarded as a matter of personal preference. His claims are clear, and these claims are verified by his resurrection. We may refuse his offer of salvation, but this would be unwarranted in light of the facts. Eternal life in God's Kingdom rests on our positive acceptance of Jesus' message.

Summary

Many scholars, especially since the time of the Enlightenment, have attempted to dismiss the historical knowledge of miracles. Many other scholars have shown that such critical attempts are incorrect. In particular, these critical dismissals of the miraculous have failed to allow for the possibility that God exists and that he acted in history in order to perform a miracle by a power superior to that of the laws of nature.

By investigating this issue, we found that there are at least two independent lines of evidence pointing to the fact that Jesus' resurrection can be known as a miracle, caused by God. Both approaches have in common the coupling of this event itself with additional data, revealing that God did miraculously raise Jesus.

Proceeding prospectively from the validity of theistic argumentation to Jesus' resurrection shows that this event was orderly and purposeful, in keeping with God's attributes and the nature of the universe, and that it served to verify a theistic message. Likewise arguing retrospectively by combining Jesus' unique resurrection with his unique theistic claims points to the probability of the validity of his theistic world-view.[31]

Although our treatment of these two lines of evidence was brief, they reveal a strong case for Christian theism. Other arguments are also corroborative,[32] but these are sufficient for our purposes to show that God did act in history to raise his Son Jesus from the dead. As such we may know, according to probability, that Jesus' resurrection was a miracle performed by God in a theistic universe.

Thus it may be asserted that naturalism is incorrect. It is in error in that it does not take into account a large portion of reality. In particular, it fails to deal with theology and the part of man which was created in God's image. In spite of the popularity of naturalism, it is one of the greatest superstitions of our time.[33] Indeed, we have seen that this is a theistic universe where God has acted by raising his Son Jesus, in order to call men unto himself by faith. Such is rejected by many modern thinkers, yet it remains firmly established by the known facts. Eternity itself hangs in the balance.

THIRTEEN

Conclusion:
Jesus' Burial Shroud

PERSONS WHO HAVE NOT studied the issue in any great detail have differing responses to the question of the authenticity of the Shroud of Turin. Some react too piously and pray to the Shroud or attribute miracle-working powers to it. Others question the Shroud by raising doubts concerning all "church relics." Still others betray their naturalistic bias by denying all supernatural implications without a fair investigation.

It should be evident to the reader that a careful study of the facts ultimately disproves each of these positions. It provides no backing whatsoever to religious enthusiasts who view the Shroud as an object of worship or endow it with special miraculous powers.

Concerning whether the Shroud should be viewed simply as a church relic, an important distinction must be made. The issue is not whether the Shroud is a relic, but whether its authenticity can be affirmed according to the evidence. In other words, regardless of what we should call the Shroud, the more important question is whether the evidence indicates that it is

175

authentic. If it is, then its credibility is not diminished because some relics have not been authentic. Thus the evidence for the Shroud's authenticity must still be explained honestly.

Being Honest with the Facts

Throughout this work we have tried not only to present the known facts, but also to be cautious in our evaluation of them. It is exactly at this point that the evidence in favor of the Shroud is most impressive. Those who dismiss the existence of the supernatural are left not only to explain the origin of the image, but also to deal with the strong historical evidence which supports the resurrection. This evidence is summarized as follows.

The work of the Shroud of Turin Research Project has shown that it is highly improbable that the Shroud is a fake, created by such methods as the application of paint, dye, powder, acid, or by any type of direct contact. Numerous tests which were used to examine even the most minute molecular substances failed to discover any foreign material which could have been added to the linen cloth in order to form the image. As noted above, Heller conservatively estimates the chances of the Shroud being a fake as 1 in 10 million![1]

Similarly, direct contact theories relying on natural hypotheses are likewise very improbable. Neither fraud nor natural contact theories can account for the three-dimensional, superficial, non-directional, and pressure-independent image on the Shroud. Additional refutations are the lack of any image plateaus or saturation, the image density, shading, color, lack of distortion, as well as the thermal and soluable stability of the image.

Likewise, other natural phenomena such as vaporgraph theories also fail. Experiments reveal that sharp images are not created this way, since vapors diffuse instead of travelling in straight or parallel lines. In addition, the fact that there are no image plateaus or saturation and no capillarity or gaseous vapor diffusion on the Shroud disproves this theory, as does the color and shading of the image. The superficiality and the three-dimensional information also refute such efforts.

Even though hypotheses involving fakery and natural explanations have failed to explain the known data, we did not therefore assert that the Shroud gives evidence for a supernatural occurrence. Numerous considerations led to that conclusion in and of themselves.

One consideration is that the Shroud is genuine. The scientists on the investigating team are unanimous in concluding that the Shroud is an actual archaeological artifact. Facts such as the exact anatomical and pathological data, the first-century date of the cloth, and the absence of fakery, its correspondence to other archaeological and historical facts even in areas unknown to an ancient artist, have led to the conclusion that it is genuine. On this point, the scientists rest their conclusion on the known facts.

The other consideration is that it was found to be highly probable that the man buried in the Shroud is the same man described in the gospels as Jesus of Nazareth. This conclusion was reached through a comparison of the areas of agreement between the Shroud and Jesus' death, points which are irregularities in normal crucifixion procedure. These irregularities include the severe beating, the crown of thorns, the absence of broken ankles, the post-mortem lance wound, and the presence of blood and watery fluid. Other irregularities are the individual burial, the fine linen shroud, the hasty burial, and the absence of decomposition. The Shroud not only agrees with the gospel accounts on these and other irregularities, but it also does not contradict the gospels at any particular point. This leads to a high probability that Jesus of Nazareth and the man buried in the Shroud are the same person. This conviction is strengthened by the fact that the Shroud is not a recently discovered artifact which happens to have an image that looks like Jesus. Rather the Shroud has been regarded down through the centuries as his actual burial garment long before it could be scientifically examined.

Thus the facts point strongly to the two conclusions that the Shroud is an actual archaeological artifact, and that it is Jesus' burial garment. The Shroud thus reveals some important facts about the physical causes for Jesus' death. It is most evident that Jesus died of asphyxiation complicated by congestive heart failure caused by the rigors of crucifixion. The post-mortem blood flow from the side wound was most likely caused by the Roman lance entering the chest and the right side of the heart, while the watery fluid proceeded from the upper pleural cavity, and perhaps the pericardium.

Testing by Heller and Adler, whereby the oxidation and dehydration process present in the Shroud image was reversed, indicated that the image fibrils reacted as if they were caused by heat. Other tests such as that by Gilbert and Gilbert, have revealed that the most likely cause for the formation of the Shroud image was a heat or light scorch. After many sensitive tests, including fluorescence, visible and infrared spectroscopy, spectrometry, and reflectance, the evidence indicates that such a heat or light scorch is the probable cause of the Shroud image.[2] This was also verified by the fact that the properties of a scorch actually include a number of the properties of the Shroud image. The image's superficiality, the lack of plateaus or saturation, the thermal and soluable stability, and the coloration are all very difficult to explain by other hypotheses. As Rogers and Jumper conclude, "that the 'body' image is chemically similar to a scorch is inescapable."[3]

Such a conclusion, of course, raises the issue of what caused the image. Such a heat or light scorch is certainly not associated with dead bodies, which do not normally give off such emissions, to be sure! Yet this is what science dictates in this instance.

It is at this point that the highly probable historical evidence for Jesus' resurrection plays an important part. It has been shown from history that Jesus did rise from the dead. There is both an absence of any viable naturalistic theories, as even critics admit, and a number of known historical evidences for this event. Additionally, a strong apologetic can be made for Jesus' resurrection based only on the known historical facts which even the critics admit, which alone produces a probable case for this event.

In light of the further probability that the Shroud is the

actual burial garment of Jesus, it is also probable that the cause of the image corresponds to the historical report that Jesus rose from the dead. Such is the probable explanation for the absence of any decomposition (which indicates bodily departure), the indication that the body was not unwrapped, and the presence of this scorch from a dead body. Also, that the Shroud corresponds so closely to the gospel accounts of Jesus' death and burial is a probable indication that it also corresponds to the historical accounts of his resurrection.

In other words, the resurrection of Jesus is also the best explanation for the lack of decomposition, the absence of any unwrapping of the body, and the presence of the heat or light scorch. This is made much more highly probable by the empirical witness of history, which also verifies Jesus' resurrection from the dead. An important consideration here is that the Shroud would then constitute scientifically empirical evidence for Jesus' resurrection. This is a type of evidence which has always seemed to elude religious belief since the first century.[4]

The conclusion reached in this book is a cautious one. Although the Shroud may somehow still turn out to be inauthentic, we must decide on the evidence before us. This evidence indicates that it is very probably the actual burial garment of Jesus, an object which gives insights into Jesus' physical death and scientific evidence for his resurrection from the dead.

The remark made by Yves Delage more than eighty years ago is relevant here. Delage, professor of comparative anatomy at the Sorbonne, a member of the prestigious French Academy, and a confirmed agnostic, concluded that the Shroud was Jesus' burial garment. When he was severely criticized for this conclusion, Delage suggested that the opposition had much to do with the identity of the man. He said that

a religious question has been needlessly injected into a problem which in itself is purely scientific. . . . If instead of Christ, there were a question of some person like a Sargon, an Achilles or one of the Pharoahs, no one would have thought of making any objection. . . . I recognize Christ as a historical personage and I see no reason why anyone should be scandalized that there still exist material traces of his earthly life.[5]

In other words, if this were a purely historical question involving anyone but Jesus, the amount of evidence available concerning the Shroud would be much more than enough to identify the man. But since the individual in question is Jesus Christ, many balk at probable scientific and historical evidence, presumably because they do not like the conclusion towards which the evidence strongly points. In a modern statement similar to Delage's, the following editorial comment appeared in William F. Buckley's *National Review*:

> As for us, we fail to understand the manifest hostility toward the Shroud on the part of some Christians. Would they be equally interested, or ostensibly uninterested in a possible or probable portrait of Xerxes? of Alexander the Great? Is it possible that the details of the Shroud are just too *literal* for an enlightened liberal sensibility? Is it somehow *bad manners* to suggest that Christian claims about what happened to Jesus are, in fact, true?[6]

As noted earlier, the resurrection of Jesus is a threat to a naturalistic world-view. But even skeptics must face the facts and align themselves with the most probable view—that Jesus did rise from the dead. A fair look at the facts indicates that God did act in raising his Son from the dead.

Here again we must challenge the reader to consider the facts and base his decision on those facts. Knowledgeable persons do decide on the probabilities involved in each specific case, and these probabilities strongly favor the authenticity of the Shroud as evidence for Jesus' death and resurrection.

Spiritual Fraud

There remains one other area of fraud to be explored. One of our rules in undertaking this inquiry into the Shroud was not to rule out any miraculous or supernatural explanation for the cloth on a presumptive basis. Thus we must ask whether an evil spiritual power could have created the image in order to sow confusion, dissension, and false belief among the people of God. Obviously, this is a question which is far more important to Christian believers than it is to nonbelievers. Christians are more likely to accept the possibility that the Shroud could have any kind of spiritual origin, and, if the origin is an evil one, it is the Christian church that is the target of it. Is it possible then that the Shroud is a satanic ploy?

Many people have had their faith deepened by the Shroud, and a study of it has led some to the first steps of faith. However, it would be foolish to pretend that the spiritual atmosphere surrounding the Shroud has always been benign. Virulent hostility has often greeted the suggestion that the Shroud of Turin may be the authentic burial shroud of Jesus Christ. When Yves Delage, the agnostic French anatomist, made public his conclusion at the turn of the century that the Shroud was authentic, his learned colleagues in the French Academy heaped ridicule and abuse on him. The Shroud is also an emotional topic among Christians. In some evangelical and Catholic circles, it elicits a hostile response. Such a response is emotional—not based on an examination of the facts. However, there is a legitimate concern about misuse of the Shroud. Relics have often been abused in the history of the church, and the Shroud of Turin is potentially the greatest of relics. Many Christians are offended by the tendency of the media to play up sensationalistic aspects of the Shroud. Christians point to such effects of the Shroud, and ask whether it can be the work of God or the work of Satan.

Two things need to be said about this. Emotional reactions to the Shroud should be separated from the question of the Shroud's authenticity. If the Shroud is real, it can teach us much about Jesus. We should first determine whether it is real. Second, we should inquire into the spiritual origins of the Shroud within the context of a firm understanding of how to clearly discern the characteristics of the work of God and the work of Satan. The scripture teaches that Satan is a spoiler who perverts and twists the truth and offers a cheap and false imitation. God is the loving Creator who seeks every opportunity to bring us to himself. With that basis, we can perhaps settle whether Satan is behind the Shroud or not.

Robert Wilcox, for example, records the story of Hans Naber, a Swiss with a flair for publicity, who decided that the Shroud gives evidence that Jesus did not die on the cross. Wilcox explains that Naber reached his extraordinary conclusion through a vision—a technicolor "film of the passion." Wilcox says that the vision "went on for seven days. . . . On the seventh day, with Naber 'physically *exhausted* and on the verge of *madness*' [emphasis-author's] something even more unusual happened. . . . Jesus appeared . . . and *there were no wounds on his body*."[7] Naber's vision could hardly be from God. It conflicts with the gospels: Jesus was declared dead by both enemies and friends and his post-resurrection state included wounds that could be both seen and touched. It also conflicts with the scientific findings (see Chapter Ten). It is likewise important to note the contrast between a vision that brought Naber to exhaustion and the point of madness, and the visions given by God in scripture which enlighten, enrapture, and bless the recipient.

In another case, one of the authors (Stevenson) spent several hours with Hugh Schonfield, author of the controversial *The Passover Plot*, and was surprised to learn that he also believes the Shroud to be genuine. However, contrary to the unanimous consensus of medical experts that that man in the Shroud is dead, Schonfield insists that the Shroud is evidence that the disciples moved the body in the night and kept the Shroud to support the resurrection story. Again we find an individual who has taken the facts and twisted them in order to read into the cloth his own personal beliefs about Christ. (See Chapters Ten and Eleven.)

Wilcox also cites the case of one Ralph Graeber who interweaves the Shroud, Jesus, and Indian mysticism in a hodgepodge religion of metaphysics and science. Disgruntled with what he termed "scientific errors from the pulpit," Graeber turned to the occult and mixed prayer to Jesus with the study of Yogi Paramahansa Yogananda.[8] Cases like these can easily be classified as individual speculation, and pose no problem for scientific investigation. Neither are they problems for the Christian discerning the work of evil spirits.

There are also a few cases of out and out abuse of the Shroud. Take, for example, a full-page ad which appeared in several publications across the nation selling mini-shrouds and photos, and advising their use as a combination prayer-cloth/good-luck talisman for any problem or desire. When the ad first appeared, an evangelical group that had offered to help raise funds for the Shroud of Turin Research Project quickly backed out.

All of these examples constitute strong evidence that the Shroud has been misused throughout its known history. However, the stories merely confirm the fact that man has a baser side to his nature. He tends to believe whatever he wants.

Let us consider the common elements in all of the above examples. First, all believed or at least claimed to believe the Shroud is genuine. Second, all sought to *use* it, either to support personal beliefs, to exploit others, or to have a physical item of worship. In any case, if the Shroud is authentic, these abuses began with its authenticity and then distorted it. To a Christian, the distortion is obvious and blatant, but it *does not prove the cloth inauthentic*. In fact, the opposite may be true.

In scripture, we read that when Jesus and his disciples confronted evil spirits, those spirits seemed to proclaim the truth (Acts 16:16; Mark 5:7; Mark 1:24; Matthew 8:29). And yet since the purpose of their proclamation was to distort the truth, the spirits were silenced. Jesus himself warned that we could expect to find "tares" mixed right in with the wheat (Matthew 13:24-30). In other words, a counterfeit requires that a genuine article exist first. To use an analogy, there is no such thing as a counterfeit three dollar bill. If the Shroud was not potentially genuine, it would have no spiritual significance at all—for good or evil. Is it possible that misuse and abuse of the Shroud is merely an attempt to misplace one's focus? Certainly this type of distortion fits Satan's method of operation. It could easily account for all of the cases cited here.

On the other hand, the Shroud has unquestionably had positive spiritual effects. Wilson, the historian, says that people he met in the course of his research on the Shroud brought him from agnostic skepticism to his acceptance of orthodox Christianity.[9]

Likewise, John A.T. Robinson, noted skeptic and New Testament scholar, wrote movingly about the Shroud and faith. His remarks followed years of study of the Shroud. Bishop Robinson began his study with the conviction that the Shroud could not possibly align itself with scripture. He began by believing the Shroud a hoax and asking how it could have been forged. But later Bishop Robinson had this to say about the Shroud:

> It would not affect my faith, but it could affect my unbelief. For if in the recognition of the face and the hands and the feet and all the other wounds we, like those who knew him best, are led to say, 'It is the Lord!' (John 21:7), then perhaps we shall have to learn to count ourselves also among those who have 'seen and believed.' But that, as St. John makes clear, brings with it no special blessing (John 20:29), but rather special responsibility (John 17:18-21)."[10]

For myself (Stevenson), the Shroud has been a powerful witness to the love of Jesus Christ. During three years of study and lecturing about the Shroud, I have always identified the image as that of the "man of the Shroud." That identification will always be sufficient for me. Because I know that Jesus suffered in precisely the manner of the man of the Shroud, it matters not what others will conclude. Even if some say the Shroud is a forgery, albeit one by an artist greater than Michaelangelo himself, it still reflects in every detail what Jesus suffered on Calvary. Hence I can and do say boldly, "Look at the physical sufferings of the man of the Shroud and realize that Jesus went through that—and he said he did it for you." That is the basis for the greatest gift of love the world has ever known. That is what it cost God to save me—and to save you too.

In the spring of 1979, I was invited to lecture at a small Episcopal church in Tenafly, New Jersey. As is my custom, I spent the last five minutes or more giving my personal testimony and warning against putting one's faith in a piece of cloth. Afterward a young man and a deacon of the church approached me. He had been moved by my lecture, and wanted clarification of the "new birth" I spoke about. This man seemed to have the Shroud in a proper spiritual perspective. A year later I learned that the young man had experienced a new birth in Jesus Christ. The lecture had led him to a personal understanding of Christianity; the Shroud had been merely a vehicle for the truth. The result was that he began to study the Word, not the cloth.

These examples illustrate the right spiritual effect of the Shroud. It brings people to focus on the finished work of Calvary, not on the cloth itself. The result is spiritual fruit: changed lives. The Shroud has had this effect on many believers and non-believers throughout its history. The question is this: would Satan generate or sponsor anything that in any way could lead to salvation? Satan was defeated at the cross, a fact scripture says he is well aware of. "The devil is come down unto you having great wrath because he knoweth that he hath but a short time" (Revelation 12:12). Would Satan call attention to his own defeat? Here we must consider the fact that Satan would have portrayed not only the blood of Jesus, but also evidence for his resurrection. The New Testament asserts that both these were factors in his defeat. Philip McNair put it well: "We know that the devil can transform himself into an angel of light, but *could* he or *would* he have portrayed from painful memory that compelling face on the Turin Shroud?"[11] It is much more likely that Satan is behind the mysterious fires, controversy, and abuses of the Shroud. Such things are signs of his handiwork.

The Shroud has been misused. While this cannot be denied, misuse does not affect authenticity. If so, we would not read the Bible because it has been used in seances. Again, as mentioned earlier, the main question concerns its authenticity.

On the other hand, the Shroud can and has been used to bring the gospel to the world. It demonstrates to all the "breadth and height . . . of the love of Christ which passeth knowledge"

(Ephesians 3:18-19). Only a Christian perspective will show us the love reflected in the faint image. This can only occur if we *do* study the subject rather than reject it out of hand.

Responsible Christians must have a responsible attitude toward the Shroud—one that is true to the facts and to the Lord. If the Shroud is authentic and we ignore it, we lose a powerful testimony to the Lord's love. If it is authentic and we reject or ridicule it, the consequences are even more serious. We risk hurting the faith of weaker Christians by leaving them open to seducing spirits who pervert the truth with half-truths. The Christian community should seriously study the Shroud and make sure that such study points to the love of Jesus. Science can only go part of the way; it cannot prove irrefutably that the man of the Shroud is Jesus Christ. However, those of us who have experienced the touch of those "nail-scarred" hands can easily take the facts about the Shroud and use them to tell of his love.

The Importance of the Shroud

Some have suggested that the Shroud is yet another outstanding sign for those in the last days that Christianity is still the only true religion. As such it would take its place besides such artifacts as the Dead Sea Scrolls. Others go further and speculate that the Shroud is actually a sign that the last days are drawing near just prior to the advent of God's Kingdom. While this issue cannot be solved by the scientific investigation of the Shroud, we may arrive at some other conclusions about the significance of the Shroud.

We have concluded in this book that the Shroud provides probable evidence for the death and resurrection of Jesus which complements the already probable historical evidence for this event. As such it need not conflict with faith, which always has been and still remains a trust in God's Son, who shed his blood for our salvation. We cannot stress this point too strongly. At no point do we ever encourage faith in the Shroud. That would be idolatry.

Here we must remember that the Shroud *proves* nothing. We

still must accept Jesus' call to salvation by faith in his person and message. He died on the cross in our place to pay for our sins and rose from the dead to secure our salvation. We must still trust him for this salvation, to which only the Holy Spirit can lead us.

Again, modern man reacts against such a message. Yet the facts are plain and they clearly favor the truthfulness of Jesus' claims because he rose from the dead. Some may not like these claims, but they are not changed by our likes or dislikes. The evidence indicates that Jesus rose. We should face this fact. Contrary to what some think, Christianity is not a leap, but a faith commitment based on historically known facts.

If the Shroud is the authentic burial garment of Jesus, then God must have a purpose in preserving it at least until our day. The evidence indicates that it is authentic. Perhaps God means for the Shroud to encourage faith in an age when there are so many doubters and questioners, even among believers.

Some skeptical philosophers have long raised the question of whether there is any strong empirical evidence for theistic beliefs. The Shroud just may initiate a new interest in this question since it provides such strong corroborating evidence for a theistic world-view. What better validation could God have left than this highly probable, empirical, and historical evidence for Jesus' resurrection and the possibility of eternal life for each of us? Indeed, when skeptics asked him to verify his message, Jesus also pointed to his resurrection from the dead (Matthew 12:38-40).

Afterword

Interest in the Shroud of Turin by persons around the world has increased significantly since the 1978 exposition. One of the results of this has been a demand for opinions as to the authenticity of the cloth from those who have been closely associated with the scientific study. Many people indicate that the answer to their query about authenticity will affect their religious beliefs.

The Shroud of Turin Research Project never intended to make a determination of the validity of claims that the Shroud is the burial cloth of Jesus. Such is not within the realm of science, but may be decided by careful historical inquiry. All that was ever proposed to be done by the scientists was the most complete and impartial scientific investigation possible, under the circumstances of the study. A report of the findings was to be made first to authorities in Turin who had approved the study and then to the international press. The interpretation of the findings was intended to be left to each individual who might be concerned with it.

Habermas and Stevenson have very fairly and accurately presented that point of view. They have carefully reviewed historical aspects of the death of Christ and have included an investigation into burial customs of the Jews at that time. Reports of the several scientists who have made observations on the physical, chemical, and photographic properties of the cloth have been included, as well as reports from some nonteam members who have theories that do not conform to the findings of the majority of the scientists. Much care has been taken in analyzing theories for the formation of the image, and the merits and deficiencies of each have been objectively explored.

It was inevitable that the question of the resurrection would come up in relation to the Shroud studies. Habermas and Stevenson have faced this issue squarely and have carefully presented all possible positions. While the majority of the scientists have been reluctant to take a stand on this matter, a few of us have openly expressed our opinions that there is support for the resurrection in the things we see on the Shroud of Turin.

It is unlikely that there will ever be a positive statement from any religious organization that the Shroud of Turin is an authentic relic. This does not imply doubt or suspicion but is merely consistent with the policies of such organizations in matters of this sort. It is far better for the faithful to make their own judgment, based on factual data. This extraordinary book will be a great help to all who seek the truth.

Robert Bucklin, M.D., J.D.
Deputy Medical Examiner, Los Angeles County
Pathologist, Shroud of Turin Research Project

APPENDIX A

Summary Critiques of Alternative
Hypotheses of Image Formation

After much research on the Shroud of Turin, the most probable theory is that the image on the cloth was formed by some kind of scorching process. However, other hypotheses have been suggested to explain how the image was formed, and many of them have been popularized by non-team members. The following is a critique of these other hypotheses, based on the 1978 scientific testing and analysis. The two major sources for this critique are the project Summary Overview (SO) and the report drafted by Lawrence Schwalbe (SS). Other sources are indicated in parentheses.

1. **Fraud Hypotheses. These theories maintain that the Shroud was created by one of several forms of fakery.**
   a. *General theories of fraud which indicate that the image was created by the application of paint, dye, powder, or other foreign substance to the Shroud.*
   1. Microchemical analyses revealed no pigments, stains, powders, dyes, or painting media on the Shroud. Several such tests were performed, including photoreflectance and ultraviolet fluorescence, all agreeing that there is no fakery involved. In particular, X-ray fluorescence was considered the major test for detecting such fraud, and it revealed no foreign substance in the image area which

could account for the image itself (SS 16-17).

2. Fraud is refuted by the Shroud's three-dimensional characteristics (Jackson et. al. in Stevenson, 85-87).

3. Fakery is disproven by the superficial nature of the image (SS 11, 38).

4. There are no plateaus or saturation points on the Shroud image, as would be expected with applications of pigment, dye, etc. (SS 44).

5. The non-directionality of the image rules out brush strokes or other directional application of a foreign substance (cf. SS 29).

6. No capillary flow appears on the Shroud, which further rules out any liquid movement on the cloth (SO 4; Jumper in Stevenson, 132).

7. The 1532 fire would have caused chemical changes in organic pigments, but no such changes are visible on the Shroud (SS 28; Rogers in Stevenson, 133-134).

8. The water applied to the Shroud after the 1532 fire would also have caused chemical changes in many pigments, but none can be observed on the Shroud image (cf. SS 41).

9. The non-traditional body image (pierced wrists, a cap of thorns, and nude body) also militates against fraud.

b. *Walter McCrone: Iron oxide was used to touch up or to create the Shroud image.*

1. McCrone must account for refutations (1a:1-9) above, which invalidate his hypothesis.

2. The scientists *specifically* checked McCrone's thesis with highly sensitive microchemical tests and found that Fe_2O_3 does *not* account for the Shroud image (Pellicori, *Archaeology*, Jan-Feb, 1981; SO 5).

3. Submicron-size Fe_2O_3 has been available only within the last 200 years, making its use in medieval times impossible (SO 7).

4. McCrone's observations have not been verified by independent testing (SS 39).

c. *Joe Nickell: Various ideas that ink or powder application produced the Shroud image (see Bibliography).*

1. Refutations (1a:1-9) above invalidate Nickell's thesis.

2. Nickell's photographs were specifically tested and they failed the three-dimensional VP-8 analysis, thus indicating that, according to high probability, his methods did not create the true three-dimensional image on the Shroud (SS 37).

3. Such a method would probably involve image saturation, which would invalidate it (Jumper in Stevenson, 187).

4. Nickell's experiment could not re-create the resolution of the Shroud image (SS 37).

5. Nickell's "squeeze" method apparently is not historically verified as a known technique used before the 19th century (SS 37).

d. *"Acid-painting:" An acid or other chemical was added to cloth to produce an image.*

1. Refutations (1a:1-9) above also invalidate this thesis.

2. Experiments revealed that acid painting is not superficial. That is, the chemical does not remain only on the surface of the material (SS 34).

3. Testing also revealed that densities from such techniques differ from densities in the Shroud image (SS 34).

4. Acid-painting involves an additional consideration in that the acid must be neutralized or it will destroy the cloth (SS 34).

e. *Conclusion:*

1. "The image cannot have been a painting . . . no intentionally applied pigment was part of the original image . . . " (SO 7).

2. The "image is not due to a stain . . . as a painting media" (SO 8).

3. The Shroud "image does not reside in an applied pigment" (SS 60).

4. Even figured conservatively, it has been estimated that there is not more than 1 chance in 10 million that the Shroud is a fake (Heller interview, "20/20," ABC-TV, 4/16/81).

2. **Vaporgraph Theories.** These theories assert that the Shroud image was created by the diffusion of gases upward onto the

burial cloth from sources such as sweat, ammonia, blood, and burial spices.

1. Vaporgraphs cannot account for the three-dimensional nature of the Shroud image. (cf. Jumper in Stevenson, 184).

2. The superficial Shroud image refutes vaporgraphic theories because such gases permeate the cloth and are not superficial (SS 36, 41, 45; SO 4, 6; Jumper in Stevenson, 182-184).

3. There are no plateaus or saturation in the image, as would happen with vapor stains (Jumper in Stevenson, 183; cf. SS 44).

4. Vaporgraphs don't yield a clear image like that on the Shroud. Vapor images are comparatively unclear, since vapor does not travel upward in straight or parallel lines, but diffuses in the air (SS 36, 40, 45; Jumper in Stevenson, 186).

5. No gaseous diffusion or capillary flow can be observed on the Shroud's image fibrils. These should be present in a vaporgraph (SO 4; Rogers in Stevenson, 132).

6. Vaporgraphic images do not preserve the shading found in the Shroud image (SS 36).

7. More ammonia is needed to create a vaporgraph than would probably be available on a dead body (SS 41).

8. No foreign material is found on the Shroud image from such chemical reactions (SS 41, 45).

9. Few of these chemicals from or on the body are thermally stable, as is the Shroud image (SS 41).

10. Many of these chemicals are active in water, but the Shroud image is stable in water (SS 41).

11. Vaporgraphic theories cannot account for the transfer of the images of hair or coins (Jumper in Stevenson, 182).

Conclusion:

1. "Gas diffusion in the image formation process is not possible" (SO 8).

2. "We view the evidence to be quite conclusive in ruling out the Vignon vaporgraphic theory as an image formation hypothesis" (SS 45).

3. **Contact Theories: These hypotheses assert that the Shroud**

image is due to either natural contact with a body or by contact due to fakery.

   a. *General objections to all contact theories, natural or fake*

     1. Contact images would not be three-dimensional, thereby eliminating them as viable hypotheses (Jackson *et. al.* in Stevenson, 83-84; Jackson in Stevenson, 223).

     2. The superficial nature of the image is also a major critique of contact theories (SS 35, 44).

     3. The absence of plateaus or saturation in the Shroud image also militates against contact (SS 44).

     4. A contact image would rely on pressure. The fact that the Shroud reveals virtually the same density on the frontal and dorsal images indicates "that the contact transfer mechanism is pressure independent" (SS 45; SO 4-5), thus refuting contact mechanisms.

     5. That there are no chemicals on the Shroud is an important indicator that militates against any chemical transfer by contact (cf. SS 45-46).

     6. The shading in the Shroud image probably eliminates contact (Rogers in Stevenson, 132-133).

     7. The 1532 fire militates against the Shroud being formed by contact with "natural organic materials or reaction products . . . " (Rogers in Stevenson, 133-134).

     8. Many chemicals are water active, but the Shroud image is not (see SS 41).

     9. Resolution is still very difficult to explain by contact.

     10. The question of whether contact theories can properly explain the transfer of the hair or the coins should also be considered (see SS 45).

   b. *Direct Contact-Latent Image Hypothesis: The Shroud image is due to natural contact with a body, through which chemicals were transferred from the body, causing the image over a period of time.*

     1. This hypothesis is still shown to be untenable by refutations (3a:1-10) above, which disprove it, as some specific examples will show.

     2. The latent image form of direct .contact still cannot account for the three-dimensional image, as is even admitted (Pellicori, "Hypothesis: Body Contact Played a Major

Role in the Appearance of the Image," 11 March, 1980, 3-4). For instance, not all areas of the body (the face, for example) were contacted by the cloth, yet even these areas are found on the Shroud image. To use our example, there are no face "drop outs" in the Shroud image. Therefore, this contact theory cannot adequately explain the image (SS 44).

3. Superficiality is still a major problem for this method as well, since the Shroud image does not generally follow dips in the threads (SS 35, 44-45).

4. The Shroud image lacks saturation points or plateaus, which severely limits the time dependence of this model (SS 44).

5. The Shroud image is pressure independent, whereas this contact hypothesis would be pressure dependent, such as with the weight of the body on the dorsal image and the cloth on the frontal image being responsible for the image (SS 45; SO 4-5; Jackson et al in Stevenson 83; Jumper in Stevenson, 186-187). This is a very serious obstacle for this model.

6. There are no traces of sensitizing chemicals on the Shroud from any such contact procedures (cf. SS 35, 46).

7. It would seem that this hypothesis also cannot explain the transfer of the hair in the Shroud image (SS 45).

8. Some question the experimental method used to represent accelerated aging (SS 42-43).

9. One very strong objection to the latent image contact hypothesis is seldom mentioned. If such a reaction can normally occur between a dead body and a burial cloth, why do more burial garments also not have such an image? Many grave clothes exist, but the Shroud image is unique. No others have a body image at all.

c. *The "hot statue" and "hot flat-plate" theories. A statue or flat-plate image of a man was heated and a cloth laid across it, producing a contact or near-contact scorch.*

1. Many of the objections (3a:1-10) above still apply to these theories and thereby render them untenable.

2. The 1532 fire is very helpful here in that it did produce

a contact scorch in a variety of densities. However, ultraviolet fluorescence photographs showed that these scorched areas do fluoresce, while the body image does not, thereby revealing that they are different. There is also a color difference between the two types of fibrils (Pellicori in *Archaeology*, Jan-Feb, 1981)

3. Experiments have shown that hot statue or hot flatplate these are not superficial, thus invalidating these methods (Jumper in Stevenson, 187).

4. A major problem for a hot-statue or hot flat-plate hypothesis is the distortion that would be present in such an image. There is a distinct lack of distortion in the Shroud image (SS 33, 60; Jackson in Stevenson, 223-233).

5. Experiments revealed that such a hot-statue or hot flat-plate scorch would not produce the shading found on the Shroud (SS 33; Jackson in Stevenson, 223-233).

6. A hot-statue or hot flat-plate forgery would be very difficult to create without burning the cloth beyond recognition of any image.

7. The resolution of the Shroud image is another difficult issue for a hot-statue or hot flat-plate (SS 33, 60; Jackson in Stevenson, 223-233).

d. *Conclusion*:

1. Contact models, including those based on a latent image, generally have similar problems and have failed to satisfactorily explain the Shroud image (SS 45-46).

2. As Eric Jumper notes concerning the latent image hypothesis, "It has inherent in it the shortcomings of all contact models I have considered. . . . " (STURP memo, 12 Dec., 1979).

3. Experimental results such as the three-dimensionality of the Shroud image "eliminate the direct contact mechanism as a viable image-forming candidate" (Jackson, et. al. in Stevenson, 83).

4. Direct contact "could not have been responsible for generating the Shroud image. . . . " (Jackson in Stevenson, 223).

APPENDIX B

Evidence for the Scorch Hypothesis

As indicated in Chapter Six, the scorch hypothesis still has not solved the issues of resolution and shading. There are four important points to make on this issue. First, all other theories of image formation have these same problems. Second, all the other options have many additional problems and in much more crucial areas. The scorch hypothesis both explains the most data and has the fewest problems. Third, we need not expect all of the problems with the scorch thesis to be solved. Since we have much reason to believe that the image was probably not caused by any natural phenomena, neither should we expect to delineate a completely natural process to explain how the image was formed. Fourth, and perhaps the most important, the scientific evidence does indicate that the Shroud image is a scorch. The scorch hypothesis is not simply a theoretical model constructed to account for the data. We will review the evidence for the scorch theory below.

1. Several specialized scientific tests confirmed the thesis that the Shroud image is a scorch:
   a. Heller and Adler reversed the image process in order to ascertain the image cause. They reported that the image fibrils reacted as if they had been caused by heat (report in progress).
   b. The spectrophotometric studies of Gilbert and Gilbert have

produced strong evidence that the image is a scorch (SS 31).
c. The Summary Overview (p.5) lists several other analyses which point out the similarity between the image and scorch areas on the Shroud:

    1. Infrared spectra

    2. visible spectra

    3. X-ray fluorescence spectra

    4. ultraviolet fluorescence spectra

2. The Shroud image has a number of characteristics in common with the properties of a scorch, such as:

    a. oxidation, dehydration, and conjugation of image fibrils

    b. superficiality

    c. the absence of image plateaus or saturation

    d. thermal stability

    e. water stability

    f. coloration

3. Other theses based on fakery or natural hypotheses have failed to account for the scientific data, indicating that they are improbable alternatives (SS; SO; Stevenson; Heller and Adler report in progress).

APPENDIX C

Biblical Questions

A major question in the study of the Shroud of Turin is the correspondence between the Shroud image and the New Testament accounts of Jesus' burial. This appendix summarizes answers to some of these questions. (The topic is covered in detail in Chapter Four.)

a. *Did first-century Jews bury their dead by wrapping a Shroud lengthwise around the body?*

1. In a Qumran community cemetery, persons were found buried lying in the same position as the man in the Shroud, with elbows extended.

2. The *Code of Jewish Law*, "Laws of Mourning," states that a man executed by the government was to be buried in a single sheet (Chapter 364).

3. No New Testament text describes a wrapping like a mummy. To the contrary, Lazarus came out of the tomb under his own power, although impaired (see question *b* below). Such is not in harmony with Egyptian wrapping but is very compatible with the Shroud.

4. Even without 1-3, it could still be held that the burial depicted in the Shroud was only a temporary one because of the oncoming Sabbath. The women were returning on Sunday to finish the burial (Luke 23:54-24:1; Mark 16:1-3).

b. *The gospels speak of more than one strip of linen being used*

(Luke 24:12; John 19:40; 20:5-7), while the Shroud is only a single piece.

1. The man buried in the Shroud was apparently also wrapped in strips around the head (see question c. below), wrists, and feet, which agrees exactly with the description in John 11:44. These were in addition to the main sheet known as the Shroud. So there was more than one piece of linen used.

2. Luke (or early Christian tradition) used the singular and the plural interchangeably to describe the cloth(s) (cf. 23:53 with 24:12). Mark 15:46 and Matthew 27:59 also use the singular, apparently referring to one major sheet, as in the Shroud. The use of the plural thus apparently refers to additional strips.

c. *Was a napkin placed over the face of Jesus, or was it folded up and placed around his head?*

1. John 20:5-7 describes the napkin as being folded up and fitting around Jesus' head. John 11:44 also asserts that a napkin was tied around Lazarus' face. This twofold position supports the view that the small cloth was folded up and tied around the head.

2. The Mishnah (Shabbath 23:5) instructs Jews to tie up the chin before burying a body.

3. The "Laws of Mourning" also instruct Jews to bind up the chin of the dead person (chapters 351-352).

4. Evidence indicates that the man buried in the Shroud also has such a napkin wrapped around his head.

d. *Jewish burial practice included washing the body. Were there any exceptions?*

1. The "Laws of Mourning" explain that persons killed by the government or those who died a violent death were not to be washed. Thus Jewish customs actually would have prohibited the washing of Jesus' body (Chapter 364).

2. Even without this previous point, it could still be held that Jesus' body was not washed because of his hurried burial. [The women were returning with spices to anoint the body (Luke 24:1-4; Mark 16:1-3), and one purpose of spices was to cleanse.] The Mishnah effectively prohibited

washing bodies on the Sabbath (Shabbath 23:5).

3. The gospels never assert that Jesus' dead body was washed.

e. *What about the spices used in burying Jesus?* Since neither the gospels nor the Shroud give any specifics on how the spices were placed or even what form of spices were used, there is no contradiction. They may have been packed along each side of Jesus' body.

f. *Wasn't Jesus nailed to the cross through his palms instead of his wrists?*

1. Even apart from the Shroud, evangelical scholars have long believed that Jesus was nailed through the wrists. Nails in the palms of the hands would tear out under the weight of the body.

2. The Greek word "hand" includes the wrist, meaning that either area could be indicated without contradiction.

g. *Conclusion:* Not only are there no contradictions between the Shroud and the gospel accounts of Jesus' burial, but scripture and early Jewish tradition even support the type of burial depicted in the Shroud. At any rate, the Shroud cannot be dismissed on the grounds that it is inconsistent with scripture.

Chart 1: Spectrophotometric comparison of body image and scorches on the Shroud agree within experimental error. This indicates that the image may be a scorch.

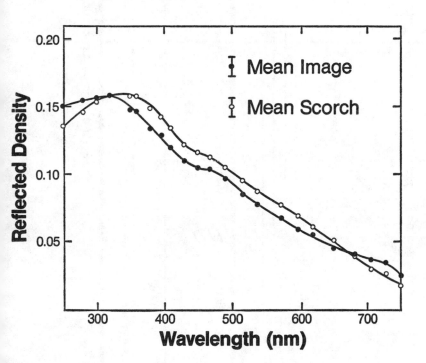

Chart 2: This diagram shows where the various Shroud experiments are located on the electromagnetic energy spectrum.

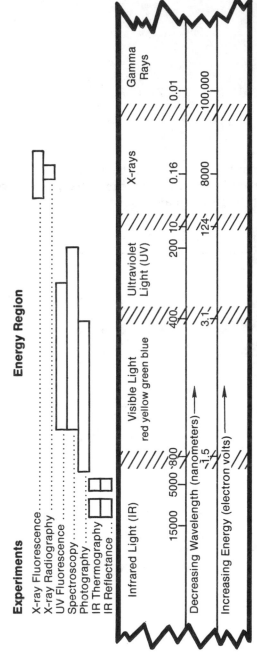

Experiments

X-ray Fluorescence
X-ray Radiography
UV Fluorescence
Spectroscopy
Photography
IR Thermography
IR Reflectance

Energy Region

Infrared Light (IR) | Visible Light red yellow green blue | Ultraviolet Light (UV) | X-rays | Gamma Rays

15000   5000   800   400   200   10   0.16   0.01

Decreasing Wavelength (nanometers) ⟶

1.5   3.1   124   8000   100,000

Increasing Energy (electron volts) ⟶

The Electromagnetic Spectrum

Notes

Chapter Two
The Shroud and History

1. Edward A. Wuenschel, *Self-Portrait of Christ: The Holy Shroud of Turin*, Esopus, New York, 1954. Ian Wilson, *The Shroud of Turin*, New York: Doubleday, 1979.

2. Wilson, *The Shroud of Turin*, pp. 104-105.

3. Ian Wilson, "The Shroud's History Before the 14th Century," in *Proceedings of the 1977 United States Conference on the Shroud of Turin*, Kenneth E. Stevenson, ed., pp. 31-49.

4. For this semi-historical account, see "The Story of the Image of Edessa" in the court history of Constantine Porphyrogenitus, printed in English translation in Appendix C of Wilson, *The Shroud of Turin*. Cf. Eusebius, *Ecclesiastical History*, Chapter XIII.

5. Marus Green, "Enshrouded in Silence," *Ampleforth Journal*, 1969, pp. 319-45.

6. Steven Runciman, "Some Reflections on the Image of Edessa," *Cambridge Historical Journal*, 1931, pp. 238-52.

7. Wilson, pp. 172-91.

8. Wilson, *Ibid*, p. 187.

9. Edward A. Wuenschel, "The Holy Shroud of Turin: Eloquent Record of the Passion," *American Ecclesiastical Review*, 1935, pp. 441-72.

10. Wilson, *Ibid*. pp. 166-70.

11. John Jackson, "Color Analysis of the Turin Shroud: A Preliminary Study," in Stevenson, pp. 190-95.

12. "The Story of the Image of Edessa," paragraph 2, in Appendix C of Wilson, *The Shroud of Turin*.

13. For a discussion, see Wilson, *Ibid.*, pp. 106-12.

14. Frei's findings are summarized in Appendix E of Wilson, pp. 293-98.

15. Gilbert Raes, "Examination of the 'Sindone,' " *Report of the Turin Commission on the Holy Shroud*, London, Screenpro Films, pp. 79-83.

16. Silvio Curto, "The Turin Shroud: Archaeological Observations Concerning the Material and the Image," *Report of the Turin Commission on the Holy Shroud*, pp. 59-73.

17. John Jackson, et. al., "The Three-Dimensional Image on Jesus' Burial Cloth," in Stevenson, p. 90.

18. Francis L. Filas, "The Dating of the Shroud of Turin from Coins of Pontius Pilate," private monograph, 1980.

19. Rachel Hachilili, "Ancient Burial Customs Preserved in Jericho Hills," *Biblical Archaeology Review*, July/August 1979, pp. 28-35.

Chapter Three

The Man Buried in the Shroud

1. Geoffrey Ashe, "What Sort of Picture?" *Sindon*, 1966, pp. 15-19.

2. For an account of the Delage affair, see John E. Walsh, *The Shroud*, New York, 1963; and Thomas Humber, *The Sacred Shroud*, New York, 1977.

3. Translation from Walsh, *The Shroud*.

4. Nicu Haas, "Anthropological Observations on the Skeletal Remains from Giv'at ha-Mivtar," *Israel Exploration Journal*, Vol. 20, No. 1-2.

5. Stewart and Coon are quoted in Robert Wilcox, *Shroud*, New York: Bantam Books, 1978, pp. 130-33.

6. Wilson, p. 47.

7. Henri Daniel-Rops, *Daily Life in the Time of Jesus*, Ann Arbor: Servant, 1981. See also Wilson, p. 47.

8. Pierre Barbet, *A Doctor at Calvary*, New York: Doubleday, 1953, pp. 91-92.

9. David Willis, cited in Wilson, pp. 38-39. See also Barbet, pp. 97-98.

10. Anthony Sava, "The Holy Shroud on Trial," in Stevenson, pp. 50-56.

11. Willis, in Wilson, pp. 43-44.

12. James Strong, *The Exhaustive Concordance of the Bible.*

13. Barbet, pp. 114-19.

14. Barbet, *Ibid.*

15. Barbet, p. 86.

16. Giulio Ricci, "Historical, Medical, and Physical Study of the Holy Shroud," in Stevenson, p. 67.

17. Paul Vignon, *The Shroud of Christ*, New Hyde Park, New York, 1970.

Chapter Four

The New Testament and the Shroud

1. Edmund Wilson, *The Scrolls from the Dead Sea*, London: Fontana, 1955, pp. 50-51.

2. *Code of Jewish Law*, "Laws of Mourning." Chapter 364. Rabbi Revkir translation.

3. See *Code of Jewish Law*, *Ibid.* See also Giulio Ricci, "Historical, Medical, and Physical Study of the Holy Shroud," in Stevenson, p. 60.

4. For comparisons of these different words, see William F. Arndt and F. Wilbur Gingrich, *A Greek-English Lexicon of the New Testament and Other Early Christian Literature*, Chicago: University of Chicago Press, 1979, pp. 177, 264, 270. Cf. John A.T. Robinson, "The Shroud of Turin and the Grave-Clothes of the Gospels," in Stevenson, p. 24.

5. Josh McDowell and Don Stewart, *Answers to Tough Questions Skeptics Ask About the Christian Faith*, San Bernardino, California: Here's Life, 1980, pp. 165-66.

6. Edward A. Wuenschel, "The Shroud of Turin and the Burial of Christ," *Catholic Biblical Quarterly 7*, 1945, and *8*, 1946.

7. For an authoritative discussion, see John A.T. Robinson, in Stevenson, pp. 23-30.

8. *Code of Jewish Law*, "Laws of Mourning," Chapters 351-352.

9. Arndt and Gingrich, pp. 270, 646.

10. John Jackson, et. al., "The Three-Dimensional Image on Jesus' Burial Cloth," in Stevenson, p. 91.

11. Robinson, in Stevenson, p. 25.

12. *Code of Jewish Law*, "Laws of Mourning," Chapter 364.

13. Robinson, in Stevenson, p. 23.

Chapter Five
Science and the Shroud: Pre-1978

1. For an account see John Walsh, *The Shroud*, and Ian Wilson, *The Shroud of Turin*.

2. Paul Vignon, *The Shroud of Christ*, New Hyde Park: University Books, 1970; and Paul Vignon and Edward Wuenschel, "The Problem of the Holy Shroud," *Scientific American*, 156(3), 162 (1937).

3. The reports of the 1969 and 1973 commissions were published together in English translation by Screenpro Films, London, in 1976. The title of the document is *Report of the Turin Commission on the Holy Shroud*.

4. Ray Rogers, "Chemical Considerations Concerning the Shroud of Turin," in Stevenson, pp. 131-35.

5. Cited in Wilson, p. 76.

6. Wilson, pp. 69-72.

7. Max Frei, "Plant Species of Pollen Samples from the Shroud," in Wilson, pp. 293-96.

8. John Jackson, et. al., "The Three-Dimensional Image on Jesus' Burial Cloth," in Stevenson, pp. 74-95.

9. Rachel Hachilili, pp. 28-35.

10. Francis L. Filas, *op. cit.*

11. Jean J. Lorre and Donald J. Lynn, "Digital Enhancement of Images of the Shroud of Turin," in Stevenson, pp. 154-80.

12. Eric Jumper, "Considerations of Molecular Diffusion and Radiation as an Image Formation Process on the Shroud," in Stevenson, pp. 182-88.

13. Geoffrey Ashe, "What Sort of Picture?" *Sindon*, 1966, pp. 15-19.

14. John Jackson, "Color Analysis of the Turin Shroud: A Preliminary Study," in Stevenson, pp. 190-95.

15. Jumper, p. 187.

16. John Jackson, "A Problem of Resolution Posed by the Existence of a Three-Dimensional Image on the Shroud," in Stevenson, pp. 223-33.

Chapter Six
Science and the Shroud: Post-1978

1. R.D. LaRue, Jr., "Tonal Distortions in Shroud Image Photographs," in Stevenson, pp. 219-221.

2. F. Ratcliff, *Scientifc American*, 226(6), 90 (1972).

3. G. Frache, E. Mari Rizzatti, and E. Mari, "A Definitive Report on the Haematological Investigations," in *Report of the Turin Commission on the Holy Shroud*, pp. 49-54.

4. J.H. Heller, and A. D. Adler, *Applied Optics*, 19, 2742 (1980).

5. L.A. Schwalbe and R.N. Rogers, "Physics and Chemistry of the Shroud of Turin: Summary of the 1978 Investigation," p. 53.

6. J.H. Heller and A.D. Adler, manuscript in preparation, cited in Schwalbe and Rogers.

7. W.C. McCrone, *Microscope 28* (3/4), 105, 115 (1980)

8. Heller and Adler, manuscript in preparation, cited in Schwalbe and Rogers.

9. R.A. Morris, L.A. Schwalbe, and J.R. London, *X-Ray Spectrometry*, 9, 40 (1980).

10. Schwalbe and Rogers, p. 39.

11. Morris, Schwalbe, and London, *Ibid*.

12. R.W. Mottern, J.R. London, R.A. Morris, *Materials Evaluation*, 38, 39 (1980).

13. R. Gilbert and M. Gilbert, *Applied Optics*, 19, 1930 (1980); S. F. Pellicori, *Applied Optics*, 19, 1913 (1980).

14. Gilbert and Gilbert, *Ibid*.

15. R.N. Rogers, "Chemical Considerations Concerning the Shroud of Turin," in Stevenson, pp. 131-35.

16. Schwalbe and Rogers, p. 38.

17. Schwalbe and Rogers, p. 34.

18. S.F. Pellicori, *op. cit.*

19. Schwalbe and Rogers, pp. 35-36.

20. Schwalbe and Rogers, pp. 43-45.

21. John Jackson, "A Problem of Resolution," in Stevenson, p. 223.

22. Paul Vignon, *The Shroud of Christ*.

23. E.J. Jumper and R.N. Rogers, "Summary Overview of Research," p. 8.

24. E.J. Jumper, "Considerations of Molecular Diffusion and Radiation as an Image Formation Process on the Shroud," in Stevenson, pp. 182-189.

25. Gilbert and Gilbert, *op. cit.*.

26. Gilbert and Gilbert, *Ibid*.

27. S.F. Pellicori and M.S. Evans, *Archeology 34* (1), 35 (1981)

28. Schwalbe and Rogers, p. 32.

29. Schwalbe and Rogers, p. 61.

30. Schwalbe and Rogers, pp. 32-33.

31. Rogers, "Chemical Considerations," in Stevenson, pp. 131-35.

32. J.P. Jackson, "A Problem of Resolution Posed by the Existence of a Three-Dimensional Image on the Shroud," in Stevenson, pp. 223-33.

33. Jackson, *Ibid*, p. 232.

34. Heller and Adler, manuscript in preparation.

Chapter Seven

Fraud and the Shroud

1. Herbert Thurston, "The Holy Shroud and the Verdict of History," *The Month* CI (1903), p. 19. Cited in Wilson, p. 53.

2. Herbert Thurston, "The Holy Shroud," *Catholic Encyclopedia*, Vol. 13, 1912 edition, pp. 762-63.

3. Ian Wilson has written the authoritative account of the early history of the Shroud in *The Shroud of Turin*.

4. "Memorandum of Pierre D'Arcis," translation from the Latin by Herbert Thurston; reprinted in Wilson, Appendix B.

5. Humber, p. 100.

6. Joe Nickell, "The Turin Shroud: Fake? Fact? Photograph," *Popular Photography*, Nov. 1979, pp. 99, 147. See also his articles in *The Humanist*, January and June, 1978.

7. Wilcox, pp. 131-32.

Chapter Eight
The Authenticity of the Shroud

1. Nelson Glueck, *Rivers in the Desert*, New York: Farrar, Straus and Cudahy, 1959, p. 31.

2. Millar Burrows, *What Mean These Stones?* New Haven: American Schools of Oriental Research, 1941, p. 1.

3. William Foxwell Albright, *Archaeology and the Religion of Israel*, Baltimore: The Johns Hopkins Press, 1953, p. 176.

4. Sir Frederick Kenyon, *The Bible and Archaeology*, New York: Harper and Brothers, Publishers, 1940, p. 279.

5. See Burrows, pp. 276-77. Burrows notes that the critical position concerning Belshazzar has changed, now recognizing his historicity as the son of Nabonides who co-reigned with his father.

6. Glueck, pp. 31-32.

7. Keith Schoville, *Biblical Archaeology in Focus*, Grand Rapids: Baker Book House, 1978, pp. 198-200.

8. F. F. Bruce, *The New Testament Documents: Are They Reliable?* Grand Rapids: Eerdmans, 1960.

9. Bruce, p. 90.

10. Bruce, Ibid; see also A.N. Sherwin-White, *Roman Society and Roman Law in the New Testament*, Oxford: Clarendon Press, 1963.

11. Vasilius Tzaferis, "Jewish Tombs at and Near Giv'at ha-Mivtar," *Israel Exploration Journal*, 1970.

12. Nicu Haas, "Anthropological Observations on the Skeletal Remains from Giv'at ha-Mivtar," *Israel Exploration Journal*, 1970. See also Paul Maier, *First Easter*, New York: Harper and Row, 1973.

13. Tacitus, *Annals*, 15.44.

14. Wilcox, pp. 129-136; cf. Wilson, p. 22.

15. Henri Daniel-Rops, *Daily Life in the Time of Jesus, op. cit.*

16. Wilson, p. 48.

17. Tacitus, 15.44.

18. Wilson, pp. 33-34. Interestingly enough, the Gospel of John states that it was the same weapon (Greek, *lonche*) which a Roman soldier thrust into Jesus' side (John 19:34). This is more properly the subject of the next chapter, but it is an appropriate parallel here as well.

19. Rachel Hachilili, pp. 28-35.

20. *Ibid.*, pp. 34-35.

Chapter Nine

Is it Jesus?

1. Ricci, p. 60.

2. Wilson, p. 38.

3. See quote from Dr. David Willis in Wilson, pp. 36-37.

4. An interview with Francis Filas in the CBN University program "Inquiry Into the Shroud of Turin," April 4, 1980.

5. Vincent J. Donovan, "The Shroud and the Laws of Probability," *The Catholic Digest*, April, 1980, pp. 49-52.

6. Donovan, *Ibid.*, p. 51; cf. Wilcox, p. 171.

7. Donovan, *Ibid.*

8. Donovan, *Ibid.*

9. Anthony Sava, "The Holy Shroud on Trial," in Stevenson, pp. 50-57.

10. Ricci, p. 67.

11. See Chapter Eleven for a detailed discussion of this point.

12. Ricci, p. 73.

Chapter Ten

The Death of Jesus: New Insights?

1. Paul Vignon, *The Shroud of Christ*, New Hyde Park: University Books, 1970.

2. See Delage's letter to Charles Richet in Wilson, pp. 33-34.

3. Pierre Barbet, *Doctor at Calvary*.

4. See Wilcox, pp. 23-25, for a discussion of Moedder's methods.

5. *Report on the Turin Commission on the Holy Shroud*, pp. 10-11.

6. See Wilson, pp. 36-44 for a discussion of Willis' unpublished findings.

7. Sava, in Stevenson, pp. 50-57.

8. Personal conversation with Robert Bucklin, April 30 and May 5, 1981.

9. Ricci, in Stevenson. p. 73.

10. Personal conversation with Robert Bucklin, May 5, 1981.

11. Jackson, et. al, in Stevenson, p. 92.

12. Personal conversation with Robert Bucklin, April 30 and May 5, 1981.

13. David Strauss, *A New Life of Jesus*, Two volumes; Edinburgh: Williams and Norgate, 1879, vol. 1, pp. 408-12.

14. Albert Schweitzer, *The Quest for the Historical Jesus*, translated by W. Montgomery from the 1906 German edition, New York: Macmillian, 1968, pp. 56-57.

15. See Edward Riggenbach, *The Resurrection of Jesus*, New York: Eaton and Mains, 1907, pp. 48-49; and James Orr, *The Resurrection of Jesus*, Grand Rapids: Zondervan, 1965, (from the 1908 edition), p. 92.

16. For example, see "The Resurrection and Biblical Criticism," *Commonweal*, Nov. 24, 1967, p. 223.

17. For examples of physicians dealing with this subject, see C. Truman Davis, "The Crucifixion of Jesus: The Passion of Christ from a Medical Point of View," in *Arizona Medicine*, March, 1965, pp. 183-87; Robert Wassenar, "A Physician Looks at the Suffering of Christ," in *Moody Monthly*, vol. 79, no.7, March, 1979, pp. 41-42; James H. Jewell, Jr. and Patricia A. Didden, "A Surgeon Looks at the Cross," in *Voice*, vol. 58, no.2, March-April, 1979, pp. 3-5. For a popular treatment, see Jim Bishop, *The Day Christ Died*, New York: Harper, 1957, pp. 312-14, 318. Bucklin also agrees with the importance of asphyxiation in crucifixion (May 5, 1981).

18. Wilcox, *Shroud*, p. 161.

19. Davis, p. 187; cf. Wilson, p. 28.

20. Personal conversation with Robert Bucklin, May 5, 1981. See also, Wilson, pp. 25-26; and Ricci, in Stevenson, pp. 58-73.

21. Wilson, pp. 44-45.

22. Wassenar, p. 42; Jewell, p. 5; cf. Davis, p. 187. See also Barbet, *Doctor at Calvary*.

23. Sava, in Stevenson pp. 51-54.

24. See Wilcox, pp. 72-73; Wilson, pp. 44-45.

25. Personal conversations with Robert Bucklin, April 30 and May 5, 1981.

26. Personal conversation with Robert Bucklin, May 5, 1981.

27. Sava, in Stevenson pp. 53-54.

28. Davis, p. 187.

29. See especially Luke 23:46; cf. also Matthew 27:50; Mark 15:37; John 19:30.

30. For instance, see Mark 10:45; Matthew 26:28.

31. For examples, see Romans 5:6-9; 1 Corinthians 15:3-4; 1 Peter 1:18-19; 1 John 1:7-10.

Chapter Eleven
The Resurrection of Jesus: New Evidence?

1. See Chapter 5, and especially appendix A for in-depth refutations of such fraud and naturalistic theories.

2. Larry Schwalbe and Ray Rogers, "Physics and Chemistry of the Shroud of Turin: Summary of the 1978 Investigation," March 27, 1981; Ray Rogers and Eric Jumper, "Summary Overview and Near Term Direction of Research," October 14, 1979; Appendix A, 1; personal conversations with John Heller, May 19, 1980; with Ray Rogers, May 21, 1980; with Eric Jumper, September 6, 1978.

3. Heller, May 19, 1980.

4. Heller, *Ibid.*; Rogers, May 21, 1980; personal conversation with Eric Jumper, Jan. 2, 1980. Cf. Ray Rogers, "Chemical Considerations Concerning the Shroud of Turin," in Stevenson, pp. 131-35; John Jackson, "A Problem of Resolution Posed by the Existence of a Three-Dimensional Image on the Shroud," in Stevenson, pp. 223-33.

5. Personal conversations with John Heller, May 19, 1980 and April 26, 1981. Heller and Adler manuscript in preparation.

6. Schwalbe and Rogers, p. 31.

7. Ray Rogers and Eric Jumper, p. 8.

8. Gary Habermas, *The Resurrection of Jesus: A Rational Inquiry*, Ann Arbor: University Microfilms, 1976.

9. For detailed refutations, see *Ibid.*, pp. 114-71.

10. A complete refutation of Hume's essay would take us beyond the scope of this chapter. For a detailed treatment, see Gary Habermas, "Skepticism: Hume," in *Biblical Errancy: An Analysis of Its Philosophical Roots*, edited by Norman L. Geisler, Grand Rapids: Zondervan, 1981.

11. William Hordern, *A Layman's Guide to Protestant Theology*, New York: Macmillan, 1955, p. 37.

12. For some examples of these liberal dismissals of alternative theories, see Habermas, pp. 292-93.

13. Raymond Brown, "The Resurrection and Biblical Criticism," in

Commonweal, Nov. 24, 1967, especially p. 233.

14. See Reginald Fuller, *The Formation of the Resurrection Narratives*, New York: Macmillan, 1971, pp. 9ff.

15. The archaeological discovery of the Nazareth decree has provided reason to believe that Jewish leaders could have killed any who were guilty of robbing graves, for instance. This slab of marble contains an edict from Caesar commanding just such action, thereby granting the authority. See Maier, pp. 119-20.

16. Fuller, p. 37.

17. See Fuller, pp. 37, 46-47.

18. This is with the exception of the third and tenth facts, which are nevertheless still supported by strong historical data. For this entire argument in expanded form, including support of these known facts and evidences, see Gary Habermas, *The Resurrection of Jesus: An Apologetic*, Grand Rapids: Baker Book House, 1980, Chapter 1.

19. William Wand, *Christianity: A Historical Religion?*, Valley Forge: Judson Press, 1972, pp. 93-94.

20. See Gary Habermas, *The Resurrection of Jesus: An Apologetic*, Chapter 1 for an expanded treatment of this additional apologetic.

21. *Ibid.* For space reasons, we cannot present expansions of these critiques and many additional ones gathered from the accepted historical facts with regard to these and other such theories. For a complete treatment, see Habermas, *The Resurrection of Jesus: A Rational Inquiry*, pp. 114-71.

22. The additional accepted facts enumerated earlier provide other significant arguments for this event, such as the other six evidences listed above.

23. See Habermas, *The Resurrection of Jesus: An Apologetic*, Chapter 1.

24. Personal conversation with Robert Bucklin, April 30, 1981.

25. Bucklin, *Ibid.* It might also be added here that the ancient theory that Jesus' body was stolen is refuted by a number of other historical points and has even been dismissed by critics. See Gary Habermas, *The Resurrection of Jesus: A Rational Inquiry*, pp. 159, 161.

26. Personal conversation with John Heller, May 19, 1980; John Heller interview, "20/20," ABC-TV, April 16, 1981.

27. Personal conversation with Robert Bucklin, April 30, 1981.

28. Bucklin, *Ibid.* It should be carefully noted here that even *if* a natural contact or vaporgraph theory could be shown to be probable,

the Shroud would still give strong evidence for Jesus' resurrection. The body exiting, as shown by the lack of any decomposition, and the body not being unwrapped, as indicated by the intact blood stains, still combines with known history and the correspondence with the gospels to reveal the probability of Jesus' resurrection from the dead. The Shroud image would *still* provide strong additional and probable testimony to the already probable historical evidence for the resurrection of Jesus.

Chapter Twelve
The Naturalism-Supernaturalism Debate

1. Hume's essay is Section X, *Enquiry Concerning Human Understanding*, 1748.

2. *Ibid.*, especially Part I.

3. John Herman Randall, Jr., *The Making of the Modern Mind*, Revised edition; Boston: Houghton Mifflin, 1940, pp. 293, 553-54.

4. David F. Strauss, *A New Life of Jesus*, Second edition; London: Williams and Norgate, 1879, vol. 1, pp. 199-201.

5. Lawrence Burkholder, Harvey Cox, and Wolfhart Pannenberg, "A Dialog on Christ's Resurrection," *Christianity Today*, vol. XII, no. 14, April 12, 1968, pp. 5-9. See especially the comments of Harvey Cox.

6. See, for example, Anthony Flew, "Miracles," in the *Encyclopedia of Philosophy*, edited by Paul Edwards, New York: Macmillan and the Free Press, 1967, vol. 5, pp. 346-53.

7. C. S. Lewis, *Miracles: A Preliminary Study*, New York: Macmillan, 1947, 1960.

8. See Habermas, "Skepticism: Hume."

9. For strong defenses of this argument, see Norman Geisler, *Christian Apologetics*, Grand Rapids: Baker Book House, pp. 237-59; Bruce Reichenbach, *The Cosmological Argument*, Springfield: Charles C. Thomas, 1972; and William Rowe, *The Cosmological Argument* Princeton: Princeton University Press, 1975.

10. For examples, see R.E.D. Clark, *The Universe: Plan or Accident?*, London: The Paternoster Press, 1961; reprinted by Zondervan, 1972; Elton Trueblood, *Philosophy of Religion*, New York: Harper, 1957, pp. 102-05.

11. Richard Swinburne, *The Existence of God*, Oxford: The Clarendon Press, 1980; Richard Swinburne, *The Concept of Miracle*, New York: Macmillan and St. Martin's Press, 1970, pp. 66-69.

12. These strong claims are validated in Geisler, especially pp. 240-41, 247-50.

13. Clark, especially pp. 196-199.

14. Again, we will not repeat the reasoning behind these attributes because this is done in much detail in the sources listed above.

15. This argument is supported at much length by Geisler, especially pp. 237-52.

16. Gary Habermas, *The Resurrection of Jesus: An Apologetic*, especially Chapter 1-3.

17. Mark 10:45; Luke 19:10.

18. Mark 13:32; Matthew 11:27.

19. Mark 2:1-12.

20. Isaiah 53; Daniel 9:24-27; Micah 5:2.

21. Matthew 19:28-30; Luke 24:47; John 6:47.

22. Especially Matthew 5:21-48; cf. Mark 3:1-6.

23. Mark 14:61-64; John 5:18, 10:33.

24. John 1:1, 20:28, 31; Romans 1:3-4; Philippians 2:11; Titus 2:13; 2 Peter 1:1.

25. Mark 2:17; 10:45; Luke 19:10, 22:29; John 12:49-50.

26. Mark 2:1-12; Matthew 11:1-6, 12:22-28, 38-40; John 5:36-37, 10:36-38.

27. For some examples, see Reginald H. Fuller, *Foundations of New Testament Christology*, New York: Charles Scribner's Sons, 1965, pp. 105-107; Rudolf Bultmann, *Theology of The New Testament*, translated by Kendrick Grobel, two volumes; New York: Charles Scribner's Sons, 1951, 1955, vol. 1, pp. 4-11.

28. Mark 8:31, 9:31, 10:33-34; etc. For a defense of the historicity of these predictions see Habermas, *The Resurrection of Jesus: An Apologetic*, especially Chapter II.

29. See Habermas, *Ibid.*, Chapters 4-5.

30. For validation of this point, see Habermas *Ibid.*, Chapters 3-5.

31. For an indepth defense of these arguments, see Habermas, *Ibid.*, Chapter II in particular.

32. An example of an additional strong argument comes from the nature of the resurrection event. It was nonrepeatable (as far as is known) and contrary to the recognized laws of nature. It is the only exception to these laws and there is no known means by which these laws might be modified or changed to account for this event, espe-

cially since Jesus rose in a glorified body, according to the eyewitnesses. These are important indications that this event was not a natural one and that Jesus was raised from the dead. Strangely enough, Hume even admitted that the resurrection of a dead man would be a miracle brought about by supernatural power (Hume, Section X, Part I). Other arguments such as fulfilled prophecy provide other compelling reasons for the validity of Christian theism.

33. Such an interesting suggestion is found in Edward M. Yoder, Jr., "The Mysterious Shroud of Turin," *Detroit News*, Nov. 29, 1979, p. 22A. Yoder is an editor with the *Washington Star*.

Chapter Thirteen
Conclusion: Jesus' Burial Shroud

1. Interview with John Heller "20/20," ABC-TV. April 16, 1981; conversation with John Heller, May 19, 1980.

2. See Appendices A and B.

3. Rogers and Jumper, pp. 5, 8.

4. It should be carefully noted that the claims put forth in this book have been couched in terms of probability. We do not pretend to have proof concerning these issues. Yet the evidence does indicate that these claims are quite probably true.

5. Wilson, pp.33-34.

6. "Notes and Asides," in *National Review*, July 7, 1978, p. 821.

7. Wilcox, pp. 60-61, 70-71.

8. Wilcox, pp. 120-21.

9. Wilson, p. 7.

10. John A. T. Robinson, "The Shroud and the New Testament," in Jennings, p. 80.

11. McNair, p. 33.

Index